BYGONE NORTHAMPTONSHIRE

NORTHAMPTON CROSS.

BYGONE NORTHAMPTONSHIRE

EDITED BY WILLIAM ANDREWS

Republished by S.R. Publishers Ltd. 1969

First published by William Andrews & Co., Hull.
Abel & Sons, Northampton
and
Simpkin, Marshall, Hamilton, Kent & Co., London

1891

© S.R. PUBLISHERS LTD. EAST ARDSLEY, WAKEFIELD, YORKSHIRE

S.B.N. 85409-565-9

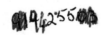
Printed in England by Kingprint Limited

Preface.

IN the following pages an attempt is made to bring together a series of chapters on the more interesting themes in the historic byways and highways of Northamptonshire.

I am greatly obliged to my contributors, and think that their articles cannot fail to interest and instruct the readers of this book.

My thanks are also due to the Rev. C. J. Gordon, M.A., and Mr. Edward Chamberlain, for the loan of illustrations, and to Mr. T. Tindall Wildridge for making some original drawings for these pages.

Mr. D. Norman, Mr. A. Chamberlain, B.A., and others, have cheerfully placed important information at my service, and otherwise helped me, and to them also I beg to tender my thanks.

In conclusion, I hope that this work may

PREFACE.

prove a welcome contribution to the literature of the Midlands. Its production has recalled many pleasant memories of my earlier life spent in that part of Old England.

WILLIAM ANDREWS.

HULL LITERARY CLUB,
November 5th, 1891.

Contents.

BYGONE NORTHAMPTONSHIRE.

Historic Northamptonshire.

By Thomas Frost.

THE reminder, to an average Northamptonshire man or woman of the present day,
that his remote ancestors were half-naked savages
at the time when Rome was the centre of the
civilisation of the ancient world, would be apt to be
regarded with feelings not very different to those
with which most of us contemplate the theory of
the evolution of our race from the simian order.
There can be no doubt, however, that the
aborigines of this island, at the time when the
Roman legions landed upon our shores, had
attained no higher degree of civilisation than
existed among the islanders of the Pacific in the
time of Captain Cook. The tribe that inhabited
what is now the County of Northampton were
called the Coritani, and that is all that is known

A

about them.   When the Romans established their
supremacy over the land, their territory was
included in the province called Flavia Cæsariensis,
and soon became intersected by roads, while
towns arose here and there in the clearings of the
great forests which then overspread so much of
the surface.

Two of the four great Roman roads which
crossed the county may still be traced.   The one
known to antiquaries as the Watling-street
entered Northamptonshire at Old Stratford, and
crossed towards Daventry ; and the Ermin-street
entered at Castor, and was continued into
Lincolnshire.   Roman remains have been found
in several places in the county.   In 1781,
extensive remains of a Roman building, including
a handsome tesselated pavement, fifty feet square,
were found at Preston Wood, in the parish of
Piddington.   At the close of the preceding
century, a similar pavement was discovered in a
meadow, about half a mile from the Watling-
street, in the parish of Heyford Nether.   About
a mile from Daventry, near a branch of the
Roman road just mentioned, is Borough Hill, the
site of the most extensive Roman camp in the
kingdom.   It is supposed that when the Roman

general, Ostorius Scapula, subdued the Coritani, he converted the northern point of the hill into a permanent camp, near which a town rose. In 1823, when the western side of the hill was excavated in the interests of archæology, the site of the Prætorium, or residence of the Roman general, was unearthed, consisting of several rooms and a bath, with a tesselated pavement, together with Roman coins, pottery, etc. The foundations of a Roman building and some interesting fragments of embossed pottery were discovered, about forty years ago, in the neighbourhood of Chipping Warden, on the site of the Roman station, Brinavis. Roman coins and pottery have also been found near Towcester.

What has been observed of the aboriginal population must be qualified, in some degree, by the change which resulted from the grafting of a people of a higher type upon the native stock. When the Romans withdrew from this country, it was invaded by warlike hordes from the shores of the Baltic, and they soon succeeded in over-running it and effecting a permanent settlement. Britons and Saxons became blended into one people, and the country of the Coritani a portion of the kingdom of Mercia. Subsequently, when the kingdoms of the Heptarchy had been united for some years under one king, and Alfred introduced the present division into counties, the town of Northampton, then called Hampton, was considered of sufficient importance to give its name to the county, with the prefix of North, to distinguish it from other places of the same name.

In the following reign, the county was overrun by the Danes, who obtained possession of North-ampton. In 918, a year afterwards, the leaders of these fierce marauders submitted to Edward, the son of Alfred; but, in 921, we find them breaking their parole, and, in conjunction with their com-patriots from Leicester, making an unsuccessful attack on Towcester. Before the close of the same year, they were defeated, and again made their submission. In 1010, another irruption of the Danes took place, under Sweyn, the father of Canute, when Northampton was burned by them, and the country around devastated to such an extent that it was nearly depopulated.

The Danes ceased to trouble the land during the reigns of the latter Saxon kings, but their plunderings and burnings had not faded out of memory when Norman William marched through England with his mail-clad host, and forced upon

the country another change of rulers. The earldom of Northampton was created by him in
favour of Waltheoff, son of the brave Siward,
Earl of Northumberland, and, in 1070, he gave
him the hand of his niece, Judith, daughter of
Odo, Earl of Albemarle. Under the successors
of the Conqueror, Northampton was on several
occasions the residence of the sovereign, and the
seat of parliaments and conferences. The first
royal visit on record was that of Henry I., in
1106, for the purpose of an interview with his
brother Robert, Duke of Normandy, for the
settlement of their differences, which, however,
remained to be disposed of in a less amicable
manner. Sixteen years later, the same monarch
revisited the town with his court, and celebrated
the festival of Easter with much pomp and
splendour of a semi-barbaric kind; and, in 1131,
a parliament or convention assembled there, in
which the barons swore fealty to the Empress
Maud of Germany, Henry's daughter and heiress.
That Maud never reigned is, however, matter of
history, being deprived of her right of succession
by Stephen.

An interesting episode of the dispute between
the Crown and the Church, or rather the priest-

hood, in the following reign was enacted in
Northampton in 1164.   Archbishop Becket
having refused his assent to the Constitutions
of Clarendon, devised in the preceding year
"for the good order of the kingdom, and for the
better defining the limits of ecclesiastical jurisdiction," he was cited to appear before the king and
his council at Northampton, there to answer the
charge of contumacy, and such others as might
be made against him.   The inquiry was opened
in the castle, to which Becket, who lodged at
the priory of St. Andrew (a portion of the site
of which is now occupied by the church of that
name), was attended through the streets by a
great concourse of the townsmen and the people
of the surrounding country.   He rode on a
sumptuously caparisoned horse, and wore his
pontifical robes, bearing a silver cross.   Thus
arrayed, he entered the hall in which the court
was held, from which the king, enraged by his
defiant bearing, immediately withdrew, followed
by his councillors.   Presently, however, the Earl
of Leicester returned, headed by the barons, and
began to read the judgment of the court.   " Son
and Earl," said Becket, interrupting him, " hear
me first.   I forbid you to judge me.   I decline

your tribunal; and refer my quarrel to the decision of the Pope. To him I appeal." He then turned and walked slowly to the door of the hall, where he mounted his horse, and rode to the priory. Thence he departed in the dead of night, disguised as a monk, and attended by two clerks and a servant, and proceeded to the coast, whence he passed over to Flanders.

The next event in the history of the county which demands our attention, is the revolt promoted by Prince Henry, when Anketil Mallory, castellan of Leicester, advanced from that town to Northampton, at the head of a considerable force, and, having defeated the burgesses who opposed him, plundered the town and carried away for ransom two hundred of the inhabitants. The outbreak was suppressed by the king, and the leaders banished to Normandy. Councils were held at Northampton in 1176 and 1177; and in 1179 a parliament, or convention of notables, sat there to amend and enforce the Constitutions of Clarendon. In the following year, another convention was held there to settle the affairs of the kingdom, prior to Henry's departure for the continent. Ten years later, Richard I. held a council at the abbey of Pipwell, within the borders of Rockingham Forest, which was attended by all the bishops and abbots of the kingdom, and many laymen of rank, the object being to make arrangements for the king's expedition against the Saracens. On his return from the East, in 1193, Richard kept the festival of Easter at the castle of Northampton, where he entertained the King of Scotland, who had made his submission to Henry II. twenty years previously.

On the death of Richard, which, as every reader of history knows, took place in Normandy, the barons held a council at Northampton, and were induced by the partisans of Prince John to take the oath of allegiance to him, though Arthur, the son of his elder brother Geoffrey, was then living. The new king was a frequent visitor to Northampton, and it is there that Shakespeare represents him as hearing the cause of the Falconbridges. With the exception of the third and fourth years of his reign, which he passed in Normandy, he visited Northampton every year, and sometimes three or four times in the same year. In 1210, he was there to receive his vassal, Llewellyn, King of Wales; and it was there, too, that he assembled a council to confer with the Papal legates for the purpose of adjusting the differences between himself and the Pope, which, however, resulted in his excommunication, no agreement being arrived at. The baronial revolt followed. The nobles had had enough of absolutism, and, assembling in arms at Stamford, marched to Brackley, where they were met by the commissioners from the king, who was then at Oxford. The concessions which they demanded being refused, the barons, under Lord Fitzwalter, advanced to Northampton, and besieged the castle, but, being unprovided with battering-rams, were unable to effect its capture. It was, however, one of the four castles placed in their hands as security for the fulfilment of the stipulations of the Great Charter. At the close of the reign trouble broke out between the garrison and the townsmen, and many of the former being slain, the soldiers, in revenge, burned a considerable portion of the town.

The political troubles of the period did not end with the reign of John. Sentence of excommunication having been pronounced by the Archbishop of Canterbury against the recent disturbers of the peace, they came to Northampton and there made their submission to the king, to whom they

surrendered the castles which they held of the
Crown.   Fresh differences arose, however, between Henry and the barons, in consequence
of his cancelling the charter of the forests, and
a baronial council was held at Northampton for
their settlement.   In 1242, when Peter of Savoy,
the Queen's uncle, was in England on a visit,
a tournament was appointed to be held at
Northampton, at which the royal guest was to
be opposed in the lists by the Earl of Norfolk,
who had acquired much distinction in the mimic
combats of which Scott has given such a vivid
picture in the romance of " Ivanhoe."   The
contemplated encounter created so much excitement, however, owing to the belief that Henry
favoured the foreigner, that the encounter was
forbidden by royal proclamation.

The contentions between the Crown and the
barons continuing, owing to the faithlessness of
the king, and the determination of the nobles to
maintain the Great Charter, the former, in 1263,
marched an army from Oxford, and attacked
Northampton, which was defended by Simon de
Montfort, son of the Earl of Leicester.   Faithless
in war as in council, Henry, being unsuccessful
in his assault of the castle, invited the barons to

a parley from the walls, and, while thus engaged, a breach was made on the opposite side, near the priory of St. Andrew, and an entrance effected. The defenders offered a desperate resistance, but the partisans of the king were the victors, and fifteen knights, with sixty gentlemen of inferior degree, were made prisoners. The war did not end here, however, and after the defeat of the king's party at the battle of Lewes, the castle of Northampton was re-taken by the barons, and their victory celebrated by a grand tournament, to which all the nobles and knights of the realm were invited.

Edward I. summoned a parliament at Northampton, shortly after his accession to the throne, and, in 1290, he spent nearly a month in the town and neighbourhood, entertaining the monks of the several orders having houses in the county three days in succession. In 1300, the court kept the festival of Christmas there, and on the death of his queen, Eleanor of Castile, her funeral cortege passed through the town on its way to Westminster, resting at the place where the cross, afterwards erected as a memorial, still stands. " The name of Edward I.," says Mr. Hartshorne, " when regarded in connection with Northampton, is linked with associations commanding an interest far beyond its vicinity, since the monument in the neighbourhood, consecrated by sincere affection to the memory of his queen, is a work not only seizing admiration by its just proportions and purity of design, but one to which all Englishmen who are imbued with a lofty feeling for art, may proudly refer as an evidence that, at this remote period, their own countrymen were capable of conceiving, as well as executing, the most sublime ideas of architectural beauty." Unfortunately, there is a less pleasant side to this picture of Edward's reign.   It is impossible to contemplate without a shudder the barbarous execution of the last sovereign of Wales, one of whose quarters was sent from Shrewsbury to Northampton, and there exposed on one of the gates ; or the execution of three hundred Jews at the latter town, on charges of clipping the coin, and, subsequently, of fifty more of those persecuted people for alleged participation in the crucifixion of a boy on Good Friday, 1279.   There is much reason to fear that such wholesale indict-ments and executions were often only pretexts for confiscating the property of the victims.

Parliament assembled at Northampton several times during the reigns of Edward III. and Richard II., the last occasion being in 1381, which was also the last time a parliament was ever held there.

During the next three-quarters of a century, there is little to record in the history of the county beyond the preaching of the Reformation by the disciples of Wickliffe, the first of whom, in Northamptonshire, was James Collyn, who was protected by John Fox, the chief magistrate of Northampton, notwithstanding the inhibition of the Bishop of Lincoln and the opposition of the clergy. But in July, 1460, the fields near Northampton were the scene of a sanguinary encounter between the armies of the contending factions of York and Lancaster. Henry VI. marched from Coventry with his forces to check the progress of the Earl of March, afterwards Edward IV., and the famous Earl of Warwick, "the king-maker," who were advancing from London; and, having crossed the Nen, occupied an advantageous position in the open, between Hardingstone and Sandyford, having the river in his rear, and strong entrenchments in front. On the morning of the 9th, the Yorkist army was seen approaching in three divisions, commanded by the Earl of March, the Earl of Warwick, and Lord Falconberg. The battle commenced next morning, when Henry's entrenchments were forced, and his army completely routed, himself taken prisoner, and several of the nobles who supported him left dead on the field. Henry entered Northampton a prisoner, and, a few days afterwards, was sent to London, and lodged in the Tower. This decisive victory gave the crown to Edward.

In 1469, a formidable insurrection having broken out in Yorkshire, a body of the insurgents marched into Northamptonshire, and defeated the king's forces at Danesmoor, near the village of Edgecote. Earl Rivers and Sir John Woodville, father and brother of the queen, were captured by the rebels at Grafton, taken to Northampton, and beheaded. More foul deeds were perpetrated on Edward's death. The Duke of Gloucester was then on the Scottish border, and the Prince of Wales at Ludlow. Earl Rivers was sent by the dowager-queen to escort the young monarch to London; but Gloucester, having arrived at Northampton on the day Rivers and his charge reached Stony Stratford, the latter joined him, and an evening was spent in con-

viviality and apparent amity. Next day, they
travelled in company towards Stony Stratford,
but, on the way, Rivers, with Lord Grey, Sir
Thomas Vaughan, and Sir Richard Hawse, were
arrested, and sent back to Northampton, whence
they were afterwards removed as prisoners to
Pontefract.

Under the Tudor regime, Northampton, in
common with many other towns in the Midland
counties, declined in importance, and, in the
reign of Henry VIII., had fallen into decay.
Whether it was due to its ceasing to be an
occasional resort of the court, or to the inter-
ference of Henry VII. with the free government
of the town, or the blighting influence of the civil
war, there is no evidence to show. Henry VIII.
passed one night in the town in 1540, on his way
to York; and it received a visit from Elizabeth
in 1564, as she travelled in stately progress to
Burghley. The queen of James I. and Prince
Henry were received in great state by the
magistrates of the town when on their way from
Edinburgh to London; and Charles I. and his
queen honoured it with a visit in 1634, when
some costly plate was presented to them.

History is not made up of royal progresses and

pageants, however, and the time was now approaching when the country was to resound once more with the tramp of hostile armies, set in motion to determine whether England should be ruled by the will of one man, or in conformity with that of the people. In that great conflict, the towns of Northamptonshire, which had become strongholds of Nonconformity, sided with the Parliament. Lord Brooke seized the castle of Northampton in 1642, and held it for the Parliament, while the ardour of the townsmen in the cause is shown by an order, preserved in the chamberlain's minutes, "That there be an assessment of £100, to be laid out in fortifying the town," and that "every householder shall send an able-bodied man every day, at one in the afternoon, to be employed on the works for the defence of the town." A letter from one Jeremiah Wharton to a friend in London states that sixty cavaliers were lodged in the castle prison, having been taken prisoners at Brackley by Lord Brooke and troops from Northampton, who defeated the company of Sir John Byron. Soon afterwards, the partisans of the king made an attack upon the town, but were beaten and driven off by the defenders, with the loss of twenty men. Then, as a news-letter in the library of the British Museum records, " The Earl of Essex came to Northampton, which was great joy and comfort to us all; but, in the night, there was a pistol-bullet shot in at his chamber window, which missed him narrowly, that caused the town to be up in arms on a sudden, but who it was that did it we cannot find as yet."

In February of the following year, Prince Rupert, with his brother Maurice and the Earl of Carnarvon, entered Northamptonshire, and, after plundering Towcester and the district round about, marched on into Warwickshire. On the 6th of May following, a battle was fought on the Town Field at Middleton Cheney, between the Royalists, commanded by the Earl of Northampton, and the Parliamentarians, in which the latter were defeated, with the loss of 217 men killed, and more than 300 taken prisoners. In August, a sharp conflict took place within a mile of Towcester, between a troop of Royalist cavalry from Banbury, who were levying contributions from the neighbourhood, and a small Parliamentarian force, the fight being maintained with obstinacy for more than half an hour. Captain Chamberlain, who commanded the Royalists, was

B

killed, as were also five of their opponents, a
much larger number being wounded. A considerable section of the royal army, commanded by
Prince Rupert, was quartered at Towcester at
this time, and frequent skirmishes took place
between the adverse forces. On one occasion, a
body of Parliamentarian cavalry, commanded by
Colonel Harvey, surprised Towcester in the night,
killed the sentries and about thirty more, and took
twenty prisoners, without the loss of a single man.
On another occasion, Captains Butler and
Wollaston, and two other captains of the Parlia-
mentary army, united their forces, and surprised
the enemy's quarters at Duncot, near Towcester,
killing about twenty, and taking thirty prisoners.

On the 18th of April, 1644, a skirmish took
place at Ashby Canons, near Towcester, between
a company of Parliamentarian infantry, sent by
the Governor of Northampton to levy contributions in the neighbourhood of Banbury, and a
body of two hundred foot and twenty horse from
the latter place, then held by the Earl of Northampton for the king. The Parliamentarians had
taken up their quarters at Canons Ashby House,
the residence of Sir John Dryden, but on the
approach of the Royalists, of which they had

timely notice, they retreated into the church.
The enemy disregarded the sacred character of
that edifice, however, and effected an entrance, on
which the defenders took refuge in the tower.
From that position their assailants were unable
to dislodge them, and, after a struggle of two
hours' duration, prepared to set fire to the building. The defenders then surrendered, and were
taken to Banbury, but, shortly afterwards, were
released by a force from Northampton.

Two months later, a Parliamentarian force from
Northampton, commanded by Major Lydcot,
attacked a body of Royalists near Towcester, and
defeated them, killing twenty-five, and taking a
great number of prisoners. These desultory
skirmishes were quickly followed by more important operations. On the 28th of June, a
Royalist army, commanded by the king in person,
was drawn up in battle array on Grimsbury Field,
near Towcester, and was faced by a Parliamentarian army, under General Waller, on the
opposite bank of the Churwell. On the following
morning, Waller having taken up a very advantageous position near Banbury, Charles drew off
towards Daventry, leaving a strong guard of
dragoons at Cropedy Bridge, to defend the

passage of the river. Waller, on attempting to force a passage across the bridge, was repulsed with great loss, and chased to a considerable distance; but he succeeded in rallying his troops again, and, having effected a junction with the forces of Major-General Brown a few days afterwards, entered Northampton on the 4th of July.

After Charles had captured Leicester, on the 31st of May, 1645, he arrived at Daventry on the 7th of June, and fixed his headquarters there, sleeping at the Wheat Sheaf Inn for six nights. His army, consisting of about 10,000 men, in nearly equal proportions of cavalry and infantry, was quartered in the neighbouring villages. He waited there several days for intelligence of the movements of Fairfax, who had drawn off from Oxford, and whose forces, he had heard, were in a disorganised condition. On the 12th, having had an alarm from a skirmishing party of Parliamentarians in the neighbourhood, he kept his army under arms all night on Borough Hill. Next morning, learning that Fairfax was at Northampton, with a larger force than had been reported to him, and in good condition, he fell back upon Market Harborough, with the intention of returning to Leicester; but the junction of

Cromwell with Fairfax forced him to abandon
that design, and risk an encounter. A decisive
battle was fought on the following day near the
village of Naseby, six miles from Harborough, in
which Charles was defeated, and forced to retreat
in confusion to Leicester, a distance of sixteen
miles. " It is not a little remarkable," observes
Mr. Baker, " that the battle which decided the
fate of the first Charles, and the last struggle of
the interregnum which terminated in the restoration of the second Charles, both took place in this
county, and within a few miles of Daventry."

The battle of Naseby was the last event of
importance which occurred within the borders of
the county during the civil war. Sir Thomas
Fairfax passed through Northampton, however,
on the 30th of December, 1647, at the head of
three regiments of cavalry and three of infantry,
escorting a treasure-chest containing £200,000 for
the Scottish army; and in the following year,
Cromwell's infantry marched through the town
without shoes and stockings, which state of
destitution moved the townsmen to send after
them to Leicester fifteen hundred pairs of those
necessary articles.   With the end of the civil war
the history of what may be called " Bygone

Northamptonshire" reaches its natural termination. The subsequent chronicles of the county are records of peaceful progress. After the restoration of monarchy, the walls of Northampton were ordered to be demolished, and as much of the castle as was not required for civil purposes was pulled down, and the site sold. The changes of the last two hundred and fifty years leave nothing to be regretted. It is better to make boots and shoes than to be the shuttle-feathers of tyrannic monarchs and lawless barons.

The Eleanor Crosses.

By the Rev. Geo. S. Tyack, b.a.

I T has been remarked by more than one historian that in the first Edward we meet the earliest king, since the Norman Conquest, who ruled this country, not as a conqueror among the conquered, but as an English-man among Englishmen. If in many of the harsher traits of his character, on the one hand, we are bound to admit that he faithfully mirrored the peculiarities of his people in his own and subsequent times, we may, on the other, surely hope that in the purity of his life and the intensity of his domestic affections, along with others of his more praiseworthy qualities, he was no less thoroughly English. The popular admiration of his contemporaries has handed down to us stories of his goodness as a son and as a father ; but of his devotion as a husband, he has himself bequeathed to us undying memorials.

The marriage of Edward was, to a large extent,

influenced by diplomatic considerations. At the age of fifteen, he received the hand of Eleanor of Castile, then only ten, and with it the undisputed title to the Duchy of Guienne, to which her brother, Alphonso X., renounced all claim in consequence of the union. Ten years later she came to England, not only to share his home, but to be his constant companion in camp as well as court, a true "help meet for him" in all the dangers and anxieties of a warlike age; for from the dry root of political expediency, sprung the fair flower of a faithful and even romantic affection.

Of the queen's devotion to her lord we have a pathetic illustration in the well-known story of her sucking the poison from his arrow-wound at Acre. That the devotion which she inspired was no less strong, the subject of this paper abundantly proves. "Living, I loved her dearly," wrote Edward to the Abbot of Cluny, "and I shall never cease to love her dead."

The golden bond thus treasured by the two was severed at a time when the king's thoughts were filled with schemes of conquest. Scotland was to be subdued, and the royal army had already advanced into the north with that pur-

pose, when the news came that Eleanor, who was
following to join it, was lying dangerously ill at
Hardeby, in Nottinghamshire. With all speed
possible her husband hurried southward to her
side ; but it was too late, the face that greeted
him was cold in death.

It was on the 28th of November 1290, after
nearly thirty years of married life (we do not count
the ten years in which they lived apart—a married
boy and girl,) that Edward was thus widowed.
The body of the queen was embalmed, the inward
parts being buried at Lincoln, the heart in the
Friars Praedicant's church, the rest in the
cathedral, while the body itself was borne in
solemn state to the Abbey at Westminster.

The sad procession began on December 4th,
and every night during the funeral march of over
one hundred and fifty miles, a halt was called, and
some spot was marked whereon a cross should
be reared to the glory of God and to the memory
of the queen. Then was the body laid, to await
the renewed journey, within some neighbouring
church or convent chapel, where flickering tapers
dimly lit the choir, in which, in silent prayer or
chanting solemn litanies for the dead, the watchers
knelt.

How many of these halts were made is uncertain. It is beyond question that crosses were erected at Geddington, Northampton, Stony Stratford, Woburn, Dunstable, St. Alban's, Waltham, Cheap, and Charing. Grantham and Stamford lay claim to the same distinction, and a few other places, which would make the total fourteen or fifteen, have been named on more doubtful authority. The city of Lincoln, where, as above stated, the queen's heart lay, also had its cross.

Certain, however, it is, that whatever the original number of these sacred memorials, three only now remain, those, namely, of Geddington, Northampton, and Waltham; and of these, it will be seen, Northamptonshire can boast the possession of two.

The tide of time, sweeping for centuries against these masterpieces of a bygone age, must undoubtedly have left its mark upon them, but it was no such gentle touch that deprived us of these and so many other similar memorials of the past. The iconoclastic zeal of a narrow and ignorant Puritanism, devoid alike of all reverence for the ancient and all love for the beautiful, this it was that " broke down all the

carved work thereof with axes and hammers."
There is a print of the Puritan era (now in the
Pennant Collection in the British museum) *
which shows us a mob in a wild frenzy, with
ropes, ladders, and hammers, wrecking the cross
in Cheapside; † and from this one instance we can
easily picture to ourselves the way in which we of
these later days have been robbed of the many
other emblems of devotion and treasures of
art, left to us by the piety and affection of
King Edward.

None of the three existing crosses have
altogether escaped the hands of the destroyer.
Geddington Cross has suffered the feast, having
lost only a very small portion at the top of the
structure; time has touched it with all gentleness,
and as the "restorer" has never interfered with
it, it has come down to us in every other respect
almost as it left the carver's hands, save for the
mellowing of age. The Northampton Cross has
also suffered decapitation, but otherwise has
had more to bear from innovators than from
destroyers; Her Majesty's justices of the peace,
under Queen Anne, took upon themselves the

* Engraved in Knight's "Old England," No. 1899.
† This destruction was not, however, due to mob violence merely, but
was the carrying out of an order of the Parliament of 1643.

improvement of the work by affixing a sundial
to each of its faces, and surmounting the whole
with a new cross out of all proportion with the
canopy-work which supported it. These additions,
no doubt well-meant, but infinitely tasteless, have
happily been removed ; would that the same were
possible with the amateur decoration which dis-
figures the base, on which some scores of visitors,
ambitious of transmitting their unknown names
to posterity, have gibbeted themselves for ever as
Goths and snobs.   The cross at Waltham, as we
now have it, is practically a new one, ill-usage and
restoration having left but little of the original ;
a second and careful restoration in recent years
(as a memorial of the jubilee of Queen Victoria
in 1887) has rendered it a fair representation of
the Eleanor Cross, but it can hardly be considered more than a nineteenth century work on
a thirteenth century model.

To the two Northamptonshire crosses, which,
together with the others, were erected between
the years 1291 and 1294, we now turn our more
particular attention.

The funeral procession, passing through Grantham and Stamford, probably made its third halt
at Geddington.   The choice of this village for

a resting-place must have been due to its possession of a royal residence, of which nothing now
remains but the tradition, and some irregular
mounds that mark the site, within a close (called
the "Hall Close") on the north side of the
churchyard. Henry II. held a council here in
1177, and again eleven years later another of
much more importance, both in its constitution
and its consequences ; for, as Stowe tells us, " he
held a parliament about the voyage into the
Holy Land, and troubled the whole land with
the paying of tithes towards it." This was
preliminary to his throwing in his lot with
Philip Augustus of France in active support of the
second crusade.

Within this manor-house, then, we can picture
the bereaved king passing the night, sometime
in the closing days of the year 1290, while the
embalmed and encoffined body of his queen rests
in the ancient church * of St. Mary Magdalene
hard by. And next morning the slow procession,
fording the Ise, here neither broad nor deep
(it is now spanned by a quaint and narrow
bridge, beside which is still a ford) winds its

---

* The church would even then be ancient, for some parts are of Saxon
workmanship.

way onward, with every outward emblem of grief, towards Northampton.

At the meeting-place of the three main streets of Geddington is a wide open space of irregular shape, and in the midst of this was raised in due time a graceful cross, the memorial of that solemn night.

On a flight of seven hexagonal steps stands a triangular column, each face of which is divided into four oblong panels by a horizontal band of moulding, and by perpendicular mouldings at the corners and in the centre, which, continued up-wards, form the shafts of canopies above. The beautifully-diapered surfaces of the panels are slightly curved, the upper ones bearing each a shield of arms. The design of the niches contain-ing the statues is peculiar ; six crocketed canopies rise from delicately formed shafts, two on each side of the triangle, but the three statues of the queen (locally called the "three weeping queens") stand, not within the arches, but facing the angles of the structure, thus having one of the corner shafts immediately in front of the figure, an arrangement which has doubtless assisted in breaking the force of the weather, and preserving the effigy within. The triangular form is pre-

GEDDINGTON CROSS.

served above by three nearly square shafts, terminating in pinnacles, whose outward faces correspond with the central shafts below; these outward faces, as well as the angles between, being relieved by pinnacle work rising from behind the niches.

So far the work is in a singularly perfect state, but the topmost stones are gone. These probably rose in a column, round which the square shafts stood like buttresses, bearing on high the small ornamental cross, with which each of these structures was surmounted.

A curious story, illustrative of the brutal sports once popular, not in bygone Northamptonshire only, but throughout bygone England, is told of the destruction of this small upper section of Geddington Cross.

On the festival of the patroness of the Parish Church, St. Mary Magdalene (July 22nd), "Geddington Feast" is held, when, among other rural sports and jollity in vogue, it was formerly the practice to fasten a squirrel to the top of the cross, to be pelted to death by the merry-makers below,* who, so the tale goes, did their part with

* For another instance of such cruel and brutalising amusements, now, happily, things of the past, see the account of the Stamford "Bull-running," in "Bygone Lincolnshire," vol. I, p. 201. (Hull, A. Brown & Sons).

such good will as not only to kill the annual squirrel, but, in the course of time, seriously to damage the chief glory of their parish. It is more than likely, however, that Puritan bigotry had done something before this in the way of removing the sign of our salvation from its place on the monument.

It will be necessary for us to say a few words on the comparisons that have been made between the still-surviving examples of the Eleanor Crosses ; but, before doing so, it will be well to consider in detail the other Northamptonshire specimen, that near the county town.

Northampton, some nineteen miles distant from Geddington, was probably the next (or fourth) resting-place of the funeral procession. The old town had long since grown used to witnessing royal state. Councils and kingly feasting had taken place here, from time to time, under almost every king since the Conquest, but never before saw it so sad a royal entry as when the funeral of Queen Eleanor swept through the streets, in the twilight of the December evening, to its temporary resting-place southward of the town. Here, at some little distance off the high road, lay on the left hand a house of Cluniac nuns, Delapre Abbey

C

by name, the chapel of which, in all probability, sheltered the bier throughout the night.

The site chosen in this instance for the memorial cross was on the highway side, facing the abbey, and overlooking the town.

The plan of Northampton Cross is octagonal, rising on seven steps, which have, unfortunately, been recently renewed. The first stage consists of eight gables of rather elaborate tracery, separated by pinnacled shafts, and bearing two shields in each face, and in the centre of each alternate face an open book upon a desk. A band of roses, delicately carved, surmounts this, above which again is a moulding ornamented with a bold indented pattern. The second stage is formed by exquisitely-worked canopies, containing four statues of the queen; here, and in almost all the tracery of this cross, foliage is largely introduced, and is most naturally and gracefully treated. The last stage of the structure, as it now stands, is quadrilateral, consisting of four traceried gables, out of which rises the broken shaft that once bore the cross.

In design, the Northampton Cross is far more elaborate, and, in the opinion of most, more graceful, than that of Geddington. The triangle is certainly not so elegant a figure on which to build as the octagon, and, from some points of view, the Geddington Cross distinctly illustrates this. Yet there is a lightness about the latter which is very attractive, arising from its small base in proportion to its height, and from the way in which one can see through the stage bearing the statues. The Nottingham Cross has, however, undoubtedly proved more suggestive to modern artists than its neighbour at Geddington has done.

The architect of the cross in the county town is said to have been John de la Battaile, while Alexander of Abingdon and William de Ireland were responsible for the execution of the work; the last-named is credited with the carving of the statues of the queen in this and several other instances. The architect of Geddington Cross is unknown; its whole design is so unlike the rest of the series of which any details have come down to us, that it seems probable that its origin was quite different, and some (judging by the style of contemporary work in Spain) have suggested that some Castilian may have designed this memorial of his royal countrywoman.*

* See an article on the Eleanor Crosses, by Mr. A. Rimmer, in the "Art Journal," of February, 1874.

With the course of this truly royal funeral we have nothing further to do ; its next resting-place is Stony Stratford, in Buckinghamshire, and so it passes beyond our province.   It will be enough for us to add that the melancholy journey was completed on December 17th, 1290, and that Charing Cross (the cross of the beloved queen, " chére reine,") marked the last halt ere that form, which all the statues tell us was both noble in stature and beautiful in feature, was at last laid to rest beneath the fretted roof of the burial-place of kings at Westminster.

As lovers of art, of antiquity, and of the Christian faith, we must needs feel indignation and regret that so many crosses, similar to those which we have attempted to describe, have been ruthlessly destroyed ; as lovers of our kind we must feel no less moved that men should have had the heart to tear down the memorials of one so worthy to be remembered.

Fotheringhay: Present and Past.

By Mrs. Dempsey.

PROBABLY no site possessing so many claims to interest from the past bears such slight present indications of what has been, so little to show the most careful observer where once stood the famous Castle of Fotheringhay, a royal residence, a state prison, the birthplace of the third Richard, and the place of execution of the beautiful, ill-fated Marie Stuart,

> "A sad prisoner, passing weary years
> In many castles, till at Fotheringhay
> The joyless life was ended."

There is an enormous, uneven mound of earth, honeycombed with rabbit-holes, and covered with grass. One side is worn into irregular ridges by which sheep sometimes climb from their quiet grazing ground in the meadow below, formerly a great yard, "half encompassing the castle." On the northern and western sides, the hill descends steeply into a long marshy pool, where ducks paddle contentedly among flags and rushes, with here and there a bright patch of blue forget-me-nots.   This is all that remains of the inner moat, sixty-six feet wide and spanned by a massive drawbridge, which, for protection and defence, once surrounded the walls.

Upon and around the mound grow very fine hawthorns, about fourteen in all, bearing in early summer pink and white May-blossoms of unusual size and beauty.   There, too, " Beside the thorn, the barren thistle springs," growing luxuriantly throughout the whole area of the castle, Scotia's emblem, " with its purple coronals and its glossy green leaves, veined with milky white," from which it receives its name of the Milk Thistle *(Carduus Marianus)*.   It may be an open question whether this or the Cotton Thistle *(Onopordium acanthium)* is *the* thistle *par excellence* of Scotland, but, beyond doubt, the Milk Thistle was the chosen emblem of Mary Queen of Scots, for, though more than three hundred years have passed, this variety is still found growing profusely about every place where she resided from Dumbarton to Fotheringhay, and the inference is that the royal captive, or some of her attendants, scattered the seed freely beyond the walls of her English prisons, as well as in the gardens of her Scottish homes.

Beyond the moat are traces of a wall, and, farther still, the Nen glides peacefully along, winding like a silver thread through "the exceeding goodly meadowes by Foderinghey," as an old chronicle has it. The river formed part of an outer moat, and also an approach by water, Edward IV. coming in this manner from Crowland, in 1469, to join his queen, then residing at Fotheringhay. This queen, Elizabeth Grey or Woodville, was secretly wooed and won by the English monarch amid the leafy shades of Grafton, not far distant. In ancient times, the Nen was crossed by a ford, and, possibly to protect this passage, the mound was first raised upon which, at a later day, the keep of the castle was built. Queen Elizabeth, in one of her progresses, made some stay at Fotheringhay, and, at her order and charges, a stone bridge of four arches was erected, upon which a tablet was placed with the inscription :—

"God save the Queen,
This bridge was made by Queen
Elizabeth, in the 15th yere of her Reygne.
A.D. 1573."

Generations passed away, the tablet was

destroyed by Cromwell's soldiers in their zealous
hatred of monarchy.   The bridge fell into decay,
and, in 1722, was re-built by a stone-mason of
Stamford.   The Nen was opened for general
navigation in 1728.

Upon the river bank stands one huge boulder,
in colour and appearance resembling limestone,
but hard as rock.   It is higher than a tall man,
and about eight feet thick.   Pieces are constantly
being chipped from the surface by visitors, and
carried away as relics.   This shapeless block
appears to be the sole fragment of the castle
masonry remaining.

Near to the castle hill stands the church, a
remarkable building in the Perpendicular style,
although the original intention of founding a
collegiate church, with cloisters, colleges, and
appropriate surroundings, was never carried out.
Above the west end of the nave rises a massive
embattled tower of two storys, surmounted by
the falcon device of the royal Yorks as a vane.

Nearly at the close of the fourteenth century,
Edmund of Langley, fifth son of Edward III.,
having re-built the ancient castle, erected a
"large and magnificent choir," at the east end of
the old church.   When he died, his son Edward,

Duke of York, continued the proposed improvements, intending to re-build the nave on a similar elaborate plan, but his death at Agincourt stopped proceedings for a time, though the work was eventually carried out, to some extent, by commissioners. When dying, Edward had directed that his burial should be at Fotheringhay. The body was conveyed to England, and laid in state at Westminster, a solemn service being performed in St. Paul's Cathedral, by order of the king. The interment took place at Fotheringhay, on December 1st, 1415, the tomb being afterwards described by the historian as "a flat, marble stone, and upon it was his image flat in brass." Successive members of the York family restored and improved other portions of the original building.

Windows of richly-stained glass were also added, no fragment of which now remains.

In the 37th year of Henry VI., Richard Plantagenet, Duke of York, was killed at the battle of Wakefield. Elated with victory, the ambitious Margaret of Angou, with unwomanly brutality, caused the head of her late opponent, encircled with a paper crown, to be placed on Micklegate Bar, overlooking the town of York.

Richard's body, with that of his second son, Edmund, the young Earl of Rutland, so barbarously murdered by Lord Clifford, were buried at Pontefract.

Time brought round the defeat of Margaret, the deposition of her husband, the coronation of the Earl of March as Edward IV., and the murder of Margaret's son. Then followed the removal of the unhappy, bereaved mother to the Tower, where her husband, Henry VI., had, with one short interval, past the last seven years of his life in bitter captivity, and where he had recently died under somewhat suspicious circumstances.

The new king, Edward, had previously caused the head of his father to be taken from the wall of York to Fotheringhay, and, in the year 1466, he transferred thither the bodies of his father and brother from Pontefract, with great pomp and ceremony.

The procession was seven days passing by easy stages to Fotheringhay, and was there met by the king and queen, the two princesses, the members of the royal household, and many others, attired in deepest mourning. The obsequies were continued for several days, and the remains were deposited in one grave in the choir, near that of the hero of Agincourt. A handsome shrine was erected by the king to their joint memory, in 1477. The wife of Richard Plantagenet survived her husband about thirty-six years, and was then buried by his side.

In the last year of Edward VI., the choir and collegiate buildings were granted to Dudley, Duke of Northumberland, and, from that time, fell gradually into decay. When Queen Elizabeth visited Fotheringhay, she found the graves of her ancestors (the Dukes of York) neglected among the ruins of the cloisters, or, as stated by Fuller, the coffins re-buried in the churchyard, without stone or memorial whatever. By the queen's command, the bodies were removed into the church, and deposited on each side of the communion table; the monuments now in existence being placed by her in memory of the illustrious dead. Over each tomb is a wooden tablet; the one on the south side bears the following inscription :—

"Edward, Duke of York, was slain at the battle of Agincourt, in the third year of Henry V., 1415."

The north tablet reads :—

"Richard Plantagenet, Duke of York, nephew to Edward,

Duke of York, and father to King Edward IV., was slain at Wakefield, in the thirty-seventh year of Henry VI., 1459, and lies buried here with Cecily, his wife.—Cecily, Duchess of York, was daughter to Ralph Neville, first Earl of Westmoreland."

The monuments bear crests, armorial devices, and various symbolical representations in common with the whole interior of the church. The one most often repeated is the device of the royal house of York, a falcon enclosed in a fetterlock. Sometimes the bird is represented as attempting to spread its wings and force the lock; and again, when the fortunes of the White Rose were in the ascendant, the falcon appeared free and the lock open.

The pavement of the church abounds in tombstones, from which the brasses have disappeared.

The original font and pulpit are still used, the latter bearing Richard III.'s badge of a boar. The font is of unique design, and a most interesting object. There is a peal of four bells, one bearing date 1595.

Fotheringhay itself is reduced from a market town of some importance in the county to a remarkably quiet and fast diminishing village. It still "is but of one street, all of stone building," and many of the houses are thatched. The

"New Inn," now a gentleman's residence, is believed to have been built by Edward IV., and was used on special occasions to supplement the accommodation of the castle.

The local belief that the Fotheringhay estate, having belonged to the Crown, will revert to the Crown again has not at present been verified; but it is a remarkable fact that very rarely has it passed from father to son for generations. Many owners have died childless, and the land has changed hands frequently simply by purchase.

It is a curious fact that while many accounts of the strength, grandeur, and magnificence of the castle have been recorded, there is no engraving, plan, or draft known to be in existence, to show the appearance of one of the most interesting places in history.

It was originally built in the reign of Stephen by Simon de St. Liz (an ancestor of Marie Stuart), who married a great-niece of William the Conqueror, and seems to have been a most unhappy possession. Its owners, with very few exceptions, "found in Fotheringhay either a troubled home, a gloomy prison, or the grave of a violent death." The last of the "luckless Balliols" to possess it was Mary of Valence,

Countess of Pembroke, whose bridegroom was killed in a tournament on the day of their marriage. "She passed the long years of her virgin-widowhood at Fotheringhay, devoting herself to the services of religion, and her fortune to the foundation of Pembroke Hall, in the University of Cambridge, to perpetuate the memory of her husband of a few hours." She was succeeded by Edmund of Langley, who rebuilt the castle, the keep being erected in the form of a horse fetterlock. His son and successor, Edward, Duke of York, perished in France, while fighting gloriously in the front rank of English archers, in 1415, and soon

"From Agincourt's victorious plain,
    They bear the fallen hero o'er the main"

to his grave in the collegiate church at Fotheringhay, which he had enlarged and adorned. His brother Richard, Earl of Cambridge, the next owner was shortly afterwards beheaded, on a charge of treason. His son Richard was the Duke of York, who was killed at Wakefield, and whose body, with that of his son Edmund, was brought to Fotheringhay for burial. Richard's wife, Cecily, daughter of the first Earl of Westmoreland, spent there nearly the whole of her sad widowhood (a period variously stated from thirty to thirty-six years), like Mary of Pembroke, and like her there too found a grave.

Conspicuous among the many sorrows of the Duchess Cecily's life must have been the terrible fate of her two little grandsons, Edward V. and his brother in the Tower. Most agonising must have been the bitterness of her grief that the cruel director of so base and treacherous a deed was her own son, born at Fotheringhay, Richard Crookback, Duke of Gloucester, afterwards Richard III., of infamous memory.

The Duchess Cecily kept the manor in her own right until the ninth year of her son Edward IV., and after that time, under successive sovereigns, it "was held in fee and right by royal hand."

Henry VII. bestowed the castle upon his wife, Elizabeth of York, as sole representative of that once-powerful family. Henry VIII. settled it on his first queen, Catherine of Arragon, who appears to have had a liking for the place, as she spent large sums of money in repairing and renovating certain portions ; but, discovering that the king had a project to keep her there in close confinement, she declared that "to Fotheringhay she would not go, unless bound with cart-ropes and carried thither." Catherine retired to Kimbolton, where she spent her life in quiet seclusion, and was afterwards buried in Peterborough Cathedral.

In the reign of Queen Mary, the castle was used as a state prison, Edward Courtney, Earl of Devon, was confined there after removal from the Tower, on a charge of being concerned in the Wyatt conspiracy.

In the autumn of 1586, the apartments in the castle which had lodged the Queen of England, were occupied by another royal lady, not this time a guest, but a prisoner, and to her Fothering-hay owes its greatest interest.

To eyes accustomed to the sunny skies of France, and the bonnie hills of Scotland, dreary must have been the prospect, across those fields in the low-lying valley of the Nen. Small wonder, in that fog-laden atmosphere, Mary suffered agonies from neuralgia and rheumatism. In October—three weeks after her arrival from Chartley—forty-six peers were appointed by Queen Elizabeth as a commission. Of these, thirty-four arrived at Fotheringhay, and were entertained at the New Inn and various other houses, as the castle precincts were filled with numerous soldiers, guards, and attendants, during the progress of the trial. Mary had been keeping her bed, and could scarcely stand; nevertheless she faced her accusers with undaunted spirit and courage, and, for two days, met their charges with a calm and dignified denial. On the second day the court broke up abruptly, and the so-called trial was ended. The commissioners met again at Westminster, when sentence of death was pronounced.

Owing to remonstrances from the King of France, Mary's life was spared for a short time, but, on February 1st, Elizabeth signed an order for the execution, suggesting that the large banqueting-hall would be a more fitting place than the court-yard. Early on Sunday morning, February 5th, the Tower executioner, and other officials, came to Fotheringhay. On Tuesday, the Earls of Kent and Shrewsbury had an interview with Mary, and informed her that her execution was to take place on the following morning, at eight o'clock.

The final scene in the grim tragedy at Fotheringhay was swiftly enacted. Unfortunate to the end, three strokes of the axe were required before the neck was severed.

D

The body was rudely wrapped in coarse cloth stripped from a billiard table, while the severed head, on a velvet cushion, was exposed in the open window of the hall to gratify the curiosity of soldiers and visitors who thronged the court-yard.

Lord Talbot mounted a swift horse and rode to tell Queen Elizabeth that her prisoner at Fotheringhay was dead.

Both head and body were carried to an upper chamber, and, after hasty and imperfect embalming, were placed in a leaden coffin ; and for six months remained unburied. James of Scotland and others petitioned Elizabeth that the body might at least receive Christian burial. She finally granted permission, and ordained that the funeral should take place at Peterborough Cathedral, with full state ceremonies. On August 1st, 1587, officers were sent from London to make arrangements, and, two days previous to the funeral, the Garter King-at-Arms, with five heralds and forty horsemen, brought to the castle a splendid car, covered with black velvet, ornamented with pennons and escutcheons, bearing the arms of Scotland, and drawn by four horses.

At ten o'clock the same night the procession started for Peterborough, attended by "a long train of mourners, both men and women, who had been faithful to the Queen of Scots in the days of her captivity, and now followed her remains as they were borne away in mock state from Fotheringhay Castle, her last prison, and the scene of her sham trial and cruel death." " It must have been a weird scene, in the dead of the night, to anyone who chanced to see that torch-light procession making its slow way along the country roads." The distance was rather more than ten miles, and the west door of the cathedral was reached between one and two o'clock in the early morning. The cortege was met by bishops and clergy, the King-at-Arms and state officers, and the coffin, which weighed nearly nine hundredweight, was at once placed in the vault prepared to receive it, in the south aisle, opposite to the tomb of Katherine of Arragon.

On Tuesday, a magnificent procession passed from the Bishop's Palace, Queen Elizabeth being represented as chief mourner by the Countess of Bedford, a crown of gold and jewels was borne on a purple velvet cushion, before a sham coffin, carried upon a bier, under a gorgeous canopy. This was placed above the vault where the real body was already laid. Impressive services and

imposing ceremonies were held over the remains
of Henry VII.'s grand-daughter. In conclusion, the burial service was read at the tomb,
and the officers of state broke their white wands
and cast them upon the coffin.

A great banquet was prepared at the Bishop's
Palace, but Mary's servants were allowed to eat
in a room apart, as they said, "their hearts were
too sad to feast, and they preferred being by
themselves, as they could not restrain their tears
from falling."

They were afterwards escorted back to
Fotheringhay, and kept in rigorous confinement
for three months, scarcely being allowed the
necessaries of life.

Mary's son, James, sent to the English court,
demanding their release, which was granted, and,
with one or two exceptions, they returned to their
native countries of France and Scotland.

No person of distinction appears to have again
resided at the castle; popular tradition tells that
one of the first acts of James, when he ascended
the English throne, was the total destruction of
the place where his mother met with so ignominious a death.

It is not correct, however, that James de-

molished the strong towers and massive walls at
Fotheringhay. Instead of destroying the castle,
James turned it to profit, by bestowing it upon
three of his courtiers, but it seems to have
been rather an encumbrance, and allowed to
fall into ruin, until a descendant of one of
these courtiers, seeing that an enormous outlay
would be required to restore the buildings, preferred to dismantle the castle, and sell not only
the contents, but also the materials of which it
was built. The lordship and manorial rights
were also sold, and changed owners frequently,
until they were bought, with the estate, by Lord
Overstone.

When the demolition of the castle was made,
about the year 1627, by order of Henry, last
Earl of Newport, a large purchaser was found in
Sir Robert Bruce Cotton, of Conington, Hunts,
who was descended from the royal family of
Scotland, and, being proud of his kinship to
Marie Stuart, endeavoured to possess himself of
every possible memento of his unfortunate relative.
He bought nearly all the old banqueting-hall.
Eleven arches and columns, which stood in the
interior, were conveyed to Conington Castle, then
being enlarged, and were built into the north and

west fronts of the ground floor. The carved oak chair used by Mary on the scaffold is still preserved in the chancel of Conington Church.

Portions of the stone were carried to Oundle, Fineshade, and other places, for building purposes, the walls, in this way, being gradually removed. In 1820, while digging out the foundations of the old banqueting-hall, a labourer found Queen Mary's ring, supposed to be her betrothal ring from Darnley, as it is engraved with the initials M.H., entwined in a true lover's knot. Inside are engraved the royal arms of Scotland, and "Henri L'Darnley." Miss Agnes Strickland conjectured that Mary wore the ring at her execution, but, falling from her finger in the agony of death, it was thrown away unseen with the bloody sawdust, to remain undiscovered for 233 years. It is now in the South Kensington Museum.

Twenty-six years after Mary's death, her son, King James, sent an autograph letter to the Dean and Chapter of Peterborough Cathedral, authorizing the removal of his mother's body to a sepulchre, befitting her rank and lineage, in Westminster Abbey, and there the body now rests, under a magnificent monument, in the south aisle of Henry VII.'s Chapel.

The Battle of Naseby.

BY EDWARD LAMPLOUGH.

AFTER the defeat of Prince Rupert's gallant army at Marston Moor, on the 2nd of July, 1664, the cause of King Charles gradually but surely declined. His Majesty had rightly estimated the crisis of the war, when he demanded of Prince Rupert the relief of York, and the defeat of Manchester's army.

Rupert's disaster lost the loyal North to the king. York surrendered ; and, one by one, the loyal fortresses fell into the hands of the Parliamentarian captains. When at the height of his prosperity, Newcastle failed to make the most effective use of the splendid material at his disposal, and in the hour of defeat he lost heart, and withdrew from the conflict.

With tireless devotion and gallantry the Cavaliers maintained the conflict, unfortunately, however, tarnishing their military fame by many

acts of license, and especially by the plundering
of the country through which they marched.

The royal commanders—Goring, Wilmot, and
Greenvil—rendered themselves especially ob-
noxious to the country people, who began to
assemble in arms for the protection of their
property from the depredations of both armies.
The members of this defensive association were
styled " Clubmen," and necessarily suffered from
the jealousy and resentment of both Parliamentarians and Cavaliers.

On the resumption of active hostilities, in 1645,
the Parliamentarians brought their famous newly-
modelled army into the field, under the command
of that brilliant soldier, Sir Thomas Fairfax.

To King Charles there remained barely a third
of his kingdom in loyal obedience, and his
widely-dispersed forces, although, perhaps, more
numerous than the Parliamentarians, were not
kept so well in hand, nor subjected to such
perfect discipline.

At first, success attended the royal plans. The
besiegers of Chester retired on the first alarm of
his advance, and on the 31st of May, he stormed
and sacked Leicester.

Fairfax had projected the relief of Taunton,

then beleagured by Greenvil, but being diverted
from this object by the command of Parliament,
he marched against the king, and on the evening
of the 13th of June, he quartered his army at
Northampton, six miles from the royal army,
which had taken up a position near the village
of Naseby, between Daventry and Harborough.

Cromwell had joined the army, having received
his commission of Lieutenant-General; and
Ireton, reconnoitering the royal army, fell upon
and forced one of the outposts.

Upon this intimation of the enemy being
within striking distance, the king called a council
of war. The first intention had been to retire
northward until the arrival of reinforcements,
but, with their usual gallantry, the Cavaliers
were eager to engage when they found the
enemy at hand, although they were outnumbered,
and conscious that the battle would, in all probability, be decisive of the struggle.

The resolution to fight was unfortunate, but—

" The Man of Blood was there, with his long essenced hair,
  And Astley, and Sir Marmaduke, and Rupert of the Rhine,"

and these gallant Cavaliers were never slow at
trying their strength against their enemies. Had

the retreat northward been continued, the royal
army would have been swollen by reinforcements
of 5000 foot and horse, including Gerrard's *corps*
of 3000. As it was, Charles had only 7,400 men
to pit against the 10,000 of Fairfax.

The Parliamentarian captains had not expected
the king to turn upon them, and abide the hazard
of the field; but on being satisfied that this was
his intention, and having obtained some information from their prisoners relative to the
number of his forces, they concluded to accept
the proffered battle. The early dawn of the
14th June beheld their serried masses in motion,
not marching to the resonant pealing of the
battle psalm, nor to the exhilarating sounds of
trumpet and drum, but pressing forward through
the grey dawn in impressive silence.

When in the vicinity of Naseby, the marching
army sighted a body of cavalry advancing under
the royal banner, and Fairfax and Cromwell
decided to form their line of battle on the spot.

Doubtless this was Rupert's reconnaissance,
and the halt of the advancing enemy induced his
rash conclusion that they were about to retreat.

The ground selected was a gentle eminence,
sloping down to, and commanding the fallow

field over which the Royalist attack would be made. With their usual deliberation and prudence, the Parliamentarians made the best of their position, and posted their twenty pieces of ordnance to command the approaches.

When Fairfax commenced his march, the Royalists were forming their line of battle on an elevation about a mile south of Harborough. Lord Astley commanded the infantry of the centre; King Charles held the reserves under his immediate orders,—they consisted of his life-guards, under the Earl of Lindsay; Rupert's regiment of foot; and the royal horse-guards, under the Earl of Lichfield. The wings consisted of cavalry, and Rupert carried his banner on the right, while Sir Marmaduke Langdale commanded the left, being assisted by Sir Henry Baird and Sir George Lisle.

To maintain his position, and compel the enemy to take the initiative, or to decline the battle, was the reasonable and prudent course that Charles should have adopted; but this course was not consistent with the character of his officers.

The impetuous Rupert was apprehensive that the enemy was retreating without risking a battle;

the rumour spread through the army; all were impatient of inaction, and anxiously awaited the first indication of the enemy's approach, too rashly concluding that the retreat had commenced.

To ascertain the state of affairs, Prince Rupert pushed on for about a couple of miles, and, drawing a rash conclusion from his hurried reconnaissance, despatched a hasty message to his royal uncle, stating that Fairfax appeared to be on the point of turning his back, and that a general advance of the royal forces would drive his army from the field.

In an unhappy hour the unfortunate monarch acceded to the wishes of his commanders, and, forsaking his position, rushed precipitately upon his fate. The ruinous consequences of defeat must have been apparent to all, yet every advantage was surrendered, and impatience and disorder reigned in the royal army. The heroism of the Cavaliers may not excuse their contempt of their adversaries, which was opposed to all reason and experience. None knew better than they that Cromwell, Fairfax, and Ireton, were not the men to retreat in confusion before an inferior army; nor were their soldiers likely, under any circumstances, to disperse without coming to blows.

"Queen Mary," was the field-word of the king's men, "God our strength," that of their opponents.

"Before the cannon was turned, or the ground chosen by the Royalists," they rashly commenced the conflict, at ten o'clock on that memorable June day.

As the Royalists closed upon their adversaries, fierce cries of exultation rolled from rank to rank, for both armies welcomed the trial at arms as though conscious that it was to prove the crown of that long, bloody waste of civil war,—the final decision of the supremacy of one of the contending parties.

Rupert commenced the battle by delivering one of his fiery charges. In vain Ireton strove to stem the rushing tide of men and horses; his squadrons were pierced, and ridden over and through. As though driven by a whirlwind, the left wing of the Parliamentarians was borne off the field in utter confusion, followed by Rupert's Cavaliers, with loose reins, wild with the excitement of pursuit, and making deadly work with pistol and rapier. Ill fared it with Ireton in the onset; his horse fell under him, slain by a shot; his face was scored by a pike, one thigh was pierced by a sword, and he fell into the hands of the "Moabites," to recover his liberty during the confusion of the later conflict.

Six cannons were captured, but the rash prince held on, chasing the fugitives to Naseby ; thus losing the golden opportunity of taking the whole of Fairfax's ordnance.   On his return, it was so well guarded by a body of Musketeers, that he failed to make any impression upon it.

With equal gallantry, Sir Marmaduke charged uphill, scourged by cannon shot, and wasted by the fire of Cromwell's Ironsides, who resorted to their carbines before falling on with the sword.

Despite the valour of the northern horse, they recoiled as Cromwell met them in full career, with his loud war-cry, "God with us."   Thus held in deadly play, the Cavaliers were shaken, and, at this crisis, a reserve of Cromwell's cavalry swept round the front of the contending warriors, and fell like a thunderclap on Sir Marmaduke's left flank.   Already staggered by Cromwell's charge, the Cavaliers were fairly over-mastered, and driven from the field.

As at Marston Moor, the infantry of the royal centre were maintaining an heroic struggle with

Fairfax and Skippon, having driven in their advanced column. It was a gallant contest for the ground, and the Cavaliers now struggled forward, anon were borne back, as the fortunes of the battle waxed and waned. The gallant, hard-fighting Fairfax was severely taxed. Skippon was wounded, but declared, when pressed to retire from the field, that "he would not stir so long as a man would stand."

Bareheaded, for he had lost his helmet in the *melee*, Fairfax dressed his lines, and strove to bear back the royal foot. Encouraged by his example, his troops clung to their ground, and the rage of battle deepened. The commander of his body-guard, Colonel Charles D'Oyley, offered to cover him with his own head-piece, and remonstrated with him for hazarding his life in the murderous hand-to-hand fight. "It is well enough, Charles," responded the hero, in kindly refusal, as he pressed forward.

Cromwell, in his care for the battle as a whole, never allowed himself to be carried away by the excitement of pursuit, and, leaving two squadrons of cavalry to pursue Langdale's horse, and prevent their rallying and resuming the conflict, he promptly proceeded to the assistance of Fairfax,

Amid the scene of carnage, one regiment of the
royal infantry was conspicuous by its unshaken
front, although D'Oyley asserted that it had
sustained two charges.   Fairfax accordingly prepared to charge the Cavaliers in front and flank.
The effect of this double charge was terrible, and
Fairfax and D'Oyley met in the heart of the
melee.   The brave young Cavalier who carried
the royal standard was slain by Fairfax, and one
of his soldiers tearing the standard from the
death-grip of the young ensign, carried it off in
triumph, loudly boasting that he had slain its late
bearer with his own hand.   Fairfax, overhearing
D'Oyley rating the boaster for his falsehood,
exclaimed, "Let him alone; I have honour
enough—let him take that honour to himself."

In this crisis of the battle, Cromwell came up
with his Ironsides, and fell upon the royal infantry,
already cruelly over-matched.   Utterly broken,
they fell in scores; many accepted quarter, and
threw down their arms, others sought to escape
from the field.   The confusion was dreadful, and
beyond the possibility of remedy.

Charles at the head of his weak reserve, beheld
the victo wrested from him, and was shaken by
the most poignant grief and despair.   He had

gallantly exerted himself to re-form his troops, and, on beholding the fatal blow with which Cromwell seconded the charges of Fairfax and D'Oyley, he attempted to charge the Ironsides at the head of his guards. Then it was that the Earl of Carneworth, swearing some round Cavaliers' oaths in the excitement of the moment, laid hands upon the king's bridle and turned his horse's head round, crying, " What, sir, would you rush upon instant death?" On beholding this apparent movement of retreat, the royal horse fled on the spur, and the field was in the hands of the Parliamentarians.

At this dark moment, Rupert came up with his disordered cavalry, thinned by their charge and by the repulse they had sustained in attempting to carry Cromwell's cannon. The king's guard also rallied, and galloped back to his succour; but Fairfax and Cromwell were re-forming their lines, in readiness to meet Rupert's attack, or to fall upon him.

Rupert's cavalry were too weak, their horses were blown by charge and pursuit, and any attempt to recover the lost field would be induced by madness and despair; yet Charles faced the Cavaliers, sword in hand, and implored them to

E

make "One charge more, and recover the day."

Nothing remained for the Royalists but to bear their monarch from that sanguinary field. That night His Majesty reached Leicester, closely followed by the cavalry of Fairfax, whose infantry appeared before the walls on the following day.

In losing this fatal battle, Charles lost his gallant little army. The slain consisted of 150 officers and 650 soldiers; the prisoners numbered 5000, including 500 officers.

The trophies and munitions of war which fell into the hands of Fairfax were numerous and valuable. Amongst them were the King's standard, 100 pairs of colours, 12 cannons, 40 barrels of powder, and 800 stands of arms.

The king's private carriage, with his cabinet, fell into the hands of his enemies, and his private letters convinced the Parliamentarians that it was impossible to confide in his honour and integrity. Selections from the letters were printed, and the national distrust of, and indignation towards, the king, increased from that day.

Truly, as Clarendon puts it, on that melancholy day of Naseby "the king and the kingdom were both lost."

The Cottage Countess.

THE Poet Laureate has given a world-wide interest to the romantic story of "The Peasant Countess" of "Burleigh House by Stamford town," in his popular poem, "The Lord of Burleigh." He relates how Henry Cecil, in the guise of a landscape-painter in humble circumstances, wooes and weds a rustic maiden, and how a shadow overcasts her bright dream when the real rank of her husband is made known to her :—

"But a trouble weighed upon her,
     And perplexed her night and morn,
With the burthen of an honour
     Unto which she was not born.
Faint she grew, and ever fainter,
     And she murmured, ' Oh, that he
Were once more that landscape-painter,
     Which did win my heart from me.'
So she drooped and drooped before him,
     Fading slowly from his side :
Three fair children first she bore him,
     Then before her time she died."

The poet tells how keenly the Lord of Burleigh mourned her loss, and that he buried her in the dress in which she was married.

The real facts, however, are not so poetical, yet Hazlitt says that the story outdoes the "Arabian Nights." The following particulars may be regarded as a correct version of this romantic tale. Henry Cecil was born in the year 1754, and was the only child of the Hon. Thomas Chambers Cecil, by his marriage with Miss Charlotte Gardner. At the age of nineteen he had lost his parents, and was the presumptive heir to his uncle's estates and the Earldom of Exeter. He was by no means popular with his uncle, and seldom troubled the inmates of Burleigh House with his presence. While still a minor he married into a good old West of England family, and his wife was a lady of great personal charms, named Emma Vernon, the only daughter of the Squire of Hornbury Hall, in the county of Worcester. The union was not a happy one, young Cecil being far from an exemplary husband. He wasted much of his time and money in gambling. After fifteen years of married life he sought and obtained a divorce. His own folly and other circumstances

rendered him a poor man, and induced him
shortly before the time he obtained a divorce to
quit the society of those in his rank of life, and
settle down in one of the secluded villages in
Shropshire. He selected Bolas Magna, a charming little place, nestling among apple orchards
and green lanes. Here he was known as John
Jones, and was lost to the fashionable world, out
of sight and out of mind. For a short time he
lodged at the village hostelry, freely conversing
with the customers who came at night to smoke
their pipes and drink their beer. The days he
spent in sketching the pretty bits of scenery in
the district.

The noisy life of an inn soon palled upon him,
and he sought lodgings at some of the farm-
houses, but his search was almost futile, as he
was viewed with much suspicion; indeed, some
went so far as to hint that he was a highwayman.
The honest country folk failed to discover any
visible means of his making money, although they
saw that he spent it pretty freely. He at last
procured lodgings at the dwelling of a labourer
called Hoggins, and soon made himself a favourite
in the humble household. Cecil appears to have
been anticipating the day when he would be a

free man, and, even before he had obtained a
divorce, he paid some attention to an attractive
young woman named Taylor.   She, however,
being engaged, did not favour his suit.   He then
made love to Sarah Hoggins, the daughter of his
landlady—a young, comely, honest girl, who
reciprocated his affection.   Her mother was
doubtful about the matter, feeling that the
marriage of her girl with a stranger was a step
that might lead to serious results, and she had a
lingering suspicion that there might be some
truth in the rumour of her lodger being a highwayman.   The father was more favourably
inclined; he saw that the man had plenty of
money, and it was a golden opportunity not
to be missed, and he encouraged the match.
Eventually the mother had to give way.   In
June, 1791, he obtained a divorce, and, on the
3rd of October, in the same year, in the little
church of Bolas, Henry Cecil and Sarah Hoggins
were married.   He bought a piece of land near
Hodnet, and on it built a house, the largest in
the neighbourhood.   The local tradesmen looked
upon him with mistrust, and he had to make
liberal advances of money before they would
undertake the work.   Here he lived with his

young wife, teaching her such accomplishments as she would require in her future high station. He did not, however, give any hint as to his real character. His superior manners and education, in spite of the mystery of his life, made him friends, and inspired some confidence, and caused the ratepayers to elect him to one of their parish offices. The duties of his parochial appointment took him to the sessions at Shrewsbury, where he encountered a brother magistrate, who had been an old schoolfellow, but was not recognised by him. As a proof of his disposition to oblige his friends and make himself generally useful, we have found the following anecdote more than once recorded—that "he on one occasion gratified his father-in-law by carrying a large pig to be given as a present to a neighbouring squire."

A little daughter was born at Bolas, and died after living a few days, and was buried in the churchyard, without a stone to mark her grave, which is now forgotten.

After he had been married about two years he read in a country newspaper an account of the death of his uncle, which occurred towards the close of the year 1793. Early in the following

January, he repaired, with his wife, then nineteen
years of age, to Burleigh House. He merely
told her that he had to go to a distant part of
the country, and wished to have her company.
They travelled on horseback, the wife being
seated on a pillion behind her husband, according
to the fashion of the period. They stopped
at the several noblemen's and gentlemen's seats
on their route. At last they reached Burleigh
House, where she was told that she was a
countess, and the mystery of Henry Cecil solved.

When surrounded by the titled and the great
she sighed for a humbler position, but nevertheless she made an excellent wife and mother,
and the happiness of her husband was complete.
It was of short duration, for in the flower of her
life she died, deeply lamented, on January 17th,
1797.

In addition to the first-born previously mentioned, they had a daughter and two sons. One
of the sons was the peer who succeeded his father.
Lord Burleigh settled seven hundred a year on
his wife's parents, and gave them the house he
had just vacated. The Countess was cordially
received by the Earl's relatives, and mixed in
the fashionable society of London, and won

respect and regard from all with whom she came in contact.

Lawrence painted her portrait, and she is represented with an oval countenance, and far from rustic in appearance, her face being very pleasing.

It remains to be stated, to complete the outline story of the life of Henry Cecil, that he was created a marquis, and that he married for his third wife the Dowager-Duchess of Hamilton, and died in the year 1804.

The Charnel House at Rothwell.

By Edward Chamberlain.

ROTHWELL, or Rowell as it is sometimes
called, is an ancient town in the County
of Northampton, and in Domesday Book, William
the Conqueror is mentioned as Lord of the Manor
thereof. Here are several objects of peculiar
interest, the chief of which is the venerable
church, which is dedicated to the Holy Trinity.
This is the longest parish church in the county,
being one hundred and seventy-three feet in length.
In it may be seen some old Misererean seats with
their carved oaken stalls and elbow rests ; a fine
brass to William of Rothwelle, one of the first
Romish priests who held office in the edifice; a
tomb and brass to Owen Ragsdale, who founded
Jesus Hospital ; several striking funeral monuments and hatchments ; a triple piscina (very
rarely seen) and a quadruple sedilia. The
chapel of our Ladye is still in existence but
very dilapidated, and all these show that

the church at one time was of more than local importance.

It was under this ancient edifice that a curious discovery was made, and the strange sight of a vast collection of human skulls and bones was brought to view.

In the south aisle of the church, about two hundred years ago, a grave was being dug somewhat deeper than usual, when, to the surprise of the workman, a portion of the earth gave way, and his astonishment may be better imagined than described, when he found whitherward his labours had been leading him, that other workers had been there, and other gravediggers had been preparing graves before him.

It appears to have been through this that the bones were discovered, and in the vault may be seen the hole in the roof blocked up with rough stones.

The first published record of the bones is in the " Natural History of Northamptonshire," by John Morton, M.A., issued in 1712. In section 50, chapter 8, mention is made of " men's and women's skulls in the famous charnel house at Rowell," but no particulars are given beyond the words we have quoted.

An entrance is now obtained by means of a low doorway in the south porch of the church, and a narrow winding stone stairway leads us down seventeen steps into the vault.

The sight is an extraordinary one! Shall we one day be tenants of such a resting place? The thought is not calculated to raise pleasant feelings. The bones around us, stacked pile upon pile, row upon row, and layer upon layer, with almost mathematical precision, seem confronting us on every side.

The remains do not consist of complete skeletons, but only the hardest bones in the human frame, and they are stacked round the vault in alternate layers of skulls, arm and leg bones, and so on. No small bones are seen, but some of these may be hidden beneath and at the back of the piles of larger ones.

The vault measures in length thirty feet, and is fifteen feet wide. The bones are arranged on two sides and at the farther end. They average about four feet in height, and measure from two to five feet from the front to the back of the heaps.

In Paul Cypher's "History of Rothwell," the number of skeletons is stated as 30,000.

Major Whyte Melville, in his lecture on the bones, estimates them at the same number, but Mr. Samuel Sharp, in a paper read before the Committee for Local Antiquities at Northampton, gives them as 3,000 to 4,000, which is

CHARNEL HOUSE AT ROTHWELL.

probably nearer the correct number. The remains, by their marks of decay, appear to be all of the same date, and some of the skulls are white and polished as though they had never lain in a grave. Most of them appear to be the bones of full grown men, one measured thigh bone being twenty-five inches in length, and the circumference in the smallest place over four and a half inches. It is generally supposed that some of the skulls are the remains of warriors, for on examination they appear with terrible wounds upon them.

One skull in particular has a large hole in the forehead with a smaller hole at the back, which is thought to be a wound from a lance or arrow which went through the head from front to back, causing instant death.

Another skull is seen where blood has apparently run into the fracture, thus showing that it was caused during life. It was evidently given with a sword or battle-axe, and with such force that the weapon crashed through the skull to the throat of the warrior. One striking peculiarity of the skulls is that most of them have extremely low foreheads. This shows that they were not of the highest type of human beings.

There is no trace whatever as to whence these remains have been derived, and various con-jectures have been made as to their source, which may be correct or not.

One surmise, that they were brought from the battlefield at Naseby and deposited here, is quickly disposed of. Naseby is ten miles from Rothwell, and the dead at the battle did not exceed 2,000. These were buried in pits the following day, which pits may still be seen on the battlefield.

A place of sepulture for monks has been suggested, but the number of bones and the wound marks would be against this theory. Again, it has been suggested they were the victims of a plague, but of this there is no evidence.

The most probable theory is that a number of the bones were collected after some battle or conflict, and the remainder removed from a part of the graveyard taken for secular purposes, and placed from time to time in this underground chamber. The vault has a strong stone roof, and at the farther end is a sketch on the wall, which is stated to represent the Resurrection. The vault is said to have been used for the funeral rites of the Romish Church, and would be disused when the building was changed from a Catholic to a Protestant church at the time of the Reformation. If such were the case, it would easily follow that many of the smaller and softer bones perished in course of time, or were lost in removal, while the remainder, of harder nature, stored or buried in the disused vault under

the church, have there remained until the present
time.

The view of the vault is from a photograph
which was taken by means of magnesium
ribbon. The spectator is supposed to be standing near the door, and the piles of bones on either
hand and at the farther end are plainly shown.
The marks on the vaulted roof are the initials of
visitors, who, with the candles used on these
occasions, have thus distinguished themselves.

The Gunpowder Plot.

By John T. Page.

IN the historic annals of bygone Northamptonshire, two facts in connection with the
Gunpowder Plot stand out very boldly. These
are the conception and the betrayal of the plot
by Robert Catesby and Francis Tresham respectively. Both these men were natives of
Northamptonshire, and both belonged to staunch
Roman Catholic families, but their two natures
were so widely different that while one was
determined enough to stake all on the result, the
other vacillated between the claims of relationship
and friendship, until the former overpowered him
and led him to betray the cause he had espoused.

Of the families of these two men we shall give
a very brief account, and also strive to record a
few of the more important incidents in the parts
played by Robert Catesby and Francis Tresham
in this diabolical plot.

The first Catesby of any note appears on the

F

scene in the reign of Richard III. This Sir William Catesby stands revealed to us conspicuously in many stirring scenes. He was high in favour with his royal master all through his eventful reign, and in the end fought so valiantly with him on Bosworth Field that he was beheaded at Leicester, by order of the victor, three days after that celebrated battle. His grandfather, John de Catesby, had obtained, through marriage, the whole of the lordship of Ashby St. Ledger's, which, on his death, descended to his son William. After the execution of Sir William, the estate was, for some time, taken possession of by the Crown, but eventually (in 1496) was restored to his son George. Henceforth, until the reign of James I., the Catesbys played a more or less prominent part in the politics and principal events of the time, and their zeal for the Roman Catholic cause is exemplified by the fact that, in the reign of Elizabeth, the second Sir William Catesby of the name was cited and convicted before the Court of Star Chamber on the charge of attending Mass and harbouring Jesuits.

To Robert Catesby, however, the son and heir of this Sir William, it was left to hand down the name of Catesby to an unenviable fame, and to disinherit his posterity for ever, by projecting the famous Gunpowder Plot.

Looking back into the dim recesses of the centuries when, in May, 1603, Robert Catesby first conceived the plot, we behold the man, a leader amongst his fellows for anything "requiring clearness of head and strength of will," selected to organise all the main points of his diabolical scheme. A year afterwards, in May, 1604, a house has been obtained on a lease, adjoining the Parliament Houses, and in March, 1605, we see the band of conspirators have safely stored away their barrels of powder in the vaults beneath the edifice intended for destruction. What hours of anxious care and forethought are the lot of the chief during these months of plotting! What visits to Ashby are made, and what secret meetings are organised in that room which still occupies its position over the old gateway leading to the Manor House!

At length comes the time when the blow must be struck, if at all. Parliament meets on November 5th, and all is ready—the deeply-laid plans are divulged to the chosen few, and, by the time arranged, every man is at his post, and ready to do his part to place England once more under the sway of Roman Catholicism. Need we dwell on the result—how the plot was divulged by Tresham in the words of that memorable letter to Mounteagle, and how Fawkes was captured red-handed? Early on that Tuesday morning the chief members of the band are galloping for dear life from London to Ashby. It is about six in the evening of the dull November day when the paved yard of the old Manor House echoes with the clatter of Catesby's tired steed, and in a very short time he has passed out again from beneath that quaint old gateway in the direction of Dunchurch, never more to return. Away off in Worcestershire, he, with others, eventually takes shelter in the house of Stephen Lyttleton, one of his brother conspirators, at Holbeach. The house is besieged by their pursuers, and Percy and Catesby, standing back to back, fall by the same bullet.

It was in 1439 that the estates at Rushton first came into the hands of the Tresham family, when William Tresham, afterwards Sir William, became their owner. During the reign of Edward IV., Sir Thomas Tresham, who had fought for the Lancastrians, was beheaded. The estates

were then escheated to the Crown, but, though
granted to others, they eventually, in the reign of
Henry VII., reverted to one John Tresham.
His son, Sir Thomas Tresham, was most
enthusiastic in the Catholic cause, being made
by Queen Mary, as a reward for his zeal at
her accession, Lord Prior of the newly restored
Order of Knights Hospitallers of St. John of
Jerusalem. The son of this Sir Thomas died
before his father, and the estates became the
property, at the age of fifteen, of the grandson,
Thomas Tresham, who later in life was knighted
by Queen Elizabeth at Kenilworth, and whose
remarkable career is fully dealt with in
this book in the chapter entitled: "Thomas
Tresham, and his Buildings." This poor gentleman, however, suffered great persecution in
consequence of being a Roman Catholic, and
spent much of his time in prison and much of
his money in fines. "For more than twenty years
he constantly paid into the Treasury £260 a
year, as the penalty for not going to church."
He died in September, 1605, leaving his estates
to his son Francis (one of a family of ten children),
who was at that time deeply involved in the
Gunpowder Plot.

Francis Tresham has become memorable in history as an undecided character, through not throwing his whole heart into the Plot, in furtherance of which he had contributed as much as £2,000 in money. Two of his sisters had married the Lords Stourton and Mounteagle, and it was to the latter, to whom he was much attached, that he transmitted that well-known anonymous letter on the 28th of October, 1605, which led to the discovery of the Plot.

This letter is still preserved in the State Paper Office, and the following copy, in which the original spelling is adhered to, may not be out of place here :—

"my lord   out of the love i beare to some of youere frends i have a caer of youer preseruacion therfor i would advyse yowe as yowe tender youer lyf to devyss some exscuse to shift of youer attendance at this parleament for god and man hathe concurred to punishe the wickednes of this tyme and thinke not slightlye of this advertisment but retyere youre self into youre contri wheare yowe maye expect the event in safti for thowghe theare be no apparance of anni stir yet i saye they shall receyve a terrible blowe this parleament and yet they shall not seie who hurts them this cowncel is not to be contemned becauss it maye do yowe good and can do yowe no harme for the dangere is passed as soon as yowe have burnt the letter and i hope god will give yowe the grace to mak good use of it to whose holy proteccion i comend yowe.

to the ryght honorable the lord mowteagle."

It is pretty generally accepted now that Tresham sent this letter to Mounteagle as a ruse to conceal a previous betrayal of the Plot. The way in which, on being handed in by a servant, it was ordered to be read aloud to the assembled guests, and the fact of Tresham's name not being mentioned in the original indictment against those implicated, both point pretty clearly to this solution.

Tresham was, however, thrown into the Tower on the 12th of November, and, after being examined in a strange manner on various occasions, he died in prison of a painful disease on the 23rd of December, 1605, the only one of the band of conspirators who did not suffer a violent death. He was the last Tresham who owned the estates, the present occupier being in no way related to the family.

As has been seen, Francis Tresham owned the Rushton estates for only a few months between the death of his father and his own untimely end. He was known as an earnest Roman Catholic, but he paid little attention to the estate during his father's lifetime, and on his death was too bewildered by the position in which he found himself relative to the Gunpowder Plot to leave behind him any traces of his short reign as Lord of the Manor of·Rushton.

His historical fame lies in the fact that he was the only one of the conspirators who betrayed any signs of wavering, in consequence of which we are indebted to him for the non-success of one of the most diabolical and deeply-laid plots recorded in the pages of English history.

Earls Barton Church.

By T. Tindall Wildridge.

THE advancement of the arts is almost in direct ratio to the degree of security of the nations among which they are practised. In this light, no more certain key to general historic facts can be found than in the main characteristics of architectural styles, and, inversely, in national conditions lies the explanation of those styles. With this reflection it behoves us to approach such monuments of the past as the ancient Saxon church of Earls Barton.

The verdicts given during the present century upon various remains of what may be called the English adaptation of the Byzantine style of architecture have somewhat changed in the direction of greater acknowledgment of the presence of Saxon work in fabrics previously set down as purely Norman. Rickman enumerates 120 churches of this country with Saxon traces, and there are so many others containing fragments of the Saxon period that competent examination would probably now enable his list to be greatly increased. The tower of Earls Barton is an instance; in Evans & Brittons' "Beauties of England and Wales," it is treated as being of the "early Norman style." But that day has passed away, and the sturdy old tower has taken its proper place as one of the best examples of pure Anglo-Saxon architecture which the rudeness of the style has permitted the bold renovators of every succeeding period to hand down to us. It was considered by Sir Gilbert Scott as belonging to the period anterior to the invasion of England by Sweyne; this, though apparently mere conjecture, is acceptable, as it places the relic neither among the earlier nor the latest examples prior to the Conquest.

The earliest Saxon churches had no towers, which were an importation from the Continent, upon the discovery of the part which bells might be made to play in ecclesiastic usage. That Saxon architecture was by no means stationary may be inferred from the fact that they were the later portions—the towers—which were mostly retained when the Norman picks ravenned among the Saxon churches.

It is the tower that is left of Saxon Earls
Barton. It speaks of a time when communication
with the arts of Europe was limited, when payments of money were fewer than payments in
kind, and when masonic organization was here in

EARLS BARTON CHURCH TOWER.

its infancy. Yet, comparatively, the tower is
witness to more than ordinary munificence; it is
spacious and strong, and the utmost ornament of
the conventional art of its time and place was

lavished upon it.   Whether the Normans left the tower because it was then sufficiently near being equal to the church they added to it (demolishing the rest of the early building), or because the money at their disposal would not permit of the building of a new tower, is one of many similar questions to which there can be no positive reply. Retention of earlier work is often put to the score of economy, when perhaps a truer reason may be that, devastators though the mediæval building clerics were, they retained in true taste structure of periods anterior to their own, for the world has never been without its antiquaries. They had a better knowledge of the Gothic they created than we who judge it and them, and there is fair evidence that they retained the best, while, where there is incorporation with a succeeding style, it is done with surpassing lack of inharmonious contrast and incongruity.

Earls Barton Church has been subject to a careful modern restoration, though the battlement on the tower was an egregious error. The general character of the body of the building is Early Perpendicular.   Incorporated with this work are some Norman portions: part of the chancel arch; the south door, shafted, and with

rich mouldings; and a fine arcade on both north
and south sides. Dr. Bonney judges that the
rising of the three bays on the south side towards
the east indicates that the Norman chancel was
as long as the present one; this seems to be
undeniable. It is evident that the Norman
church was most elaborate.

The Tower, Northamptonshire's most antique
gem, is built in four stages, which gradually de-
crease in size at each storey. There is the usual
long and short rustic work at the corners, formed
by stones placed alternately vertical and
horizontal. There are several unglazed windows
with round shafts. The faces of the walls are
relieved by flat pilasters running continuously
from the top of the third storey to the ground,
being interrupted by the flat cornice of each stage.
The panel spaces between the pilasters are filled
with the cement-like coating known as "pebble-
dash," or "rough cast," being a concrete of
small stones and mortar.

The ground stage is the tallest, and its pilasters
are interrupted by transverse stones, fillet-wise,
at nearly regular intervals. There are some small
semi-circular arches below the cornice of this
stage, and probably they were originally in

every panel at this part. There is a small west door with a semi-circular head, projecting key-stone to outer order, and block capitals. The capitals are relieved by a slight arcading; the inner order of the arch is hewn from a single stone. In the south side of this storey is a two-light window, which has a certain barbaric grace of its own, and is an excellent example of Saxon detail of construction. It has in the head of each arch a Greek cross, which form also appears on some of the arches in the wall. Adjoining this window is a sculptured design, which is doubtless armorial, and may be the ensign of some thane who built or contributed largely to the edifice. The second stage has the flat arches of its panels upon the lower cornice, so that they adjoin the arches of the first tier. The third stage has its arches triangular, and so arranged in double rank as to form a con-tinuous belt of lozenges round the tower. The fourth tier is short, and contains the belfry windows. Here glooms the heavy Saxon in-telligence. The pilaster panelling of the rest of the tower is a decrepit and cheap copy of classic prototypes, where wood or metal "strips" ran up the walls; but these burly pillarets supporting

diminutive arches, each rounded feebly out of a
single square block, are indigenous.　The pillars
are in groups of six, and have round capitals,
square bases, and medial fillets compressing their
waists.

Britton's "Architectural Antiquities" gives a
view of this tower which shows it suppositiously
completed ; each face is surmounted by a gable

WINDOW WITH BALUSTERS, EARLS BARTON CHURCH TOWER.

of the same proportions as the triangular arches,
and in the midst rises the spire.　This form is
seen at Sompting, in Essex, but in that tower
there is no upper cornice, though no doubt the
parapet of the Earls Barton tower is a subsequent
addition.　Whatever the original form may have
been in this respect, the general aspect of the tower

must have been, in spite of its shortcomings, one
of beauty surpassing the hideously plain towers
which rose over many a lesser manor church of
say the Decorated or Perpendicular period.   It
is, in fact, to return to the reflection with which
this article commenced, surprising to find a succession of buildings akin to this the outcome of
a period so stormy and unceasingly troubled as that
in which it was built ; and its character—in part
debased, and in part undeveloped—is that of a
people whose leisure was annexed and whose
means were absorbed by never-ending strife.

Old Fairs.

By William Sharman.

THE fairs of past time were of far more importance than those of the present day. They formed the great holiday of our forefathers. Families were united at them. Friend met friend at the fair. Acquaintance was made between stranger and stranger. News was retailed and slanders circulated. Altogether the old English fair formed a common means of communication between different parts of the country, especially in Northamptonshire, it being one of the most central of all the English counties.

Most of its ancient towns have the privilege of a fair. Towns without one are in most cases but of recent growth.

Northampton boasts of numerous fairs, especially of the one devoted to the sale of wool.

The ancient city of Peterboro' has several, but, as regards the business transacted, no fair is larger than the one held at Boughton Green,

G

a parish without a village, at the present time, even the little church itself being in ruins.

But the business done at Boughton Green fair in the past was simply enormous. Days before the fair, goods of all descriptions found their way to Northampton and the neighbouring towns, and upon the 24th of June a fair of large size was in full swing. Carts, waggons, rakes, ladders, ropes, and string, had their allotted portion of standing room in the commodious field. Immense stacks of besoms, thousands of feet of timber, and huge piles of hurdles, occupied another portion, and tempted Farmer Brown to "speculate."

Tradespeople went there to meet tradesmen of neighbouring counties. Buckinghamshire sent its wood hoops. Leicestershire its willow bowls. Kings Cliffe its noted taps, spoons, and carved ware. Banbury supplied its celebrated cakes, and Corby and Geddington, rakes and shafts. Horses, cattle, sheep, and pigs, had a day allotted for their sale. Shows, swings, stalls, and sweetmeats attracted the youngsters, whilst older people could every day have their fortune told, be cheated at thimble rig, or pay the piper in the dancing booth. So much money was taken at this

fair that on one occasion a certain Captain Slash
and a number of other reckless desperadoes decided
to attempt to secure a share of it for themselves.
So, toward midnight, when all the stall-keepers
and showmen were asleep, the band attacked the
wild beast show and liberated some of the inmates. The noise of the beasts and the screams
of the awakened stall-keepers were terrible in
the darkness, but the captain failed to secure
much of the money as one stall-keeper ran for
help from the Green to Northampton in her
night-dress, and her bags of copper and silver
tied to her. Meantime, however, the keepers of
the wild beast and others fell upon the rogues
and drove them off (when fully acquainted with
the state of affairs.)

Wellingboro', a town of 15,000 inhabitants, has
several fairs, but the chief one is that dedicated
to Saint Luke, and held in October. A hundred
years ago, when the town was not half the size it
is now, its streets, during the fair time, were
filled with merchandise. Cheese Lane was
crowded with piles of cheeses; Market Street
with cattle; Sheep Street with pens of sheep,
and Broad Green with its pleasure fair. The
inhabitants have a curious dinner called Hock

and Dough Flake, which is still very commonly eaten on the Fair Sunday. It consists of pork with a surrounding layer of flour and water mixed into a paste, interspersed with potatoes and seasoned with herbs. But even St. Luke's Fair becomes every year of less importance, and is scarcely more now than a larger market.

The village of Corby holds a fair once every twenty years. Upon the fair day, which is Whit-Monday, every visitor that enters early either pays a toll of not less than sixpence, or is chaired shoulder high through the village to find a resting-place in the old-fashioned stocks.

We might mention other fairs, but to give a good idea of one of the most ancient let us imagine ourselves at Rothwell, or Rowell, as it is more commonly called, say in the year 1790. It is a very old town, noted for its hospital, market-house, nunnery, and bone vault. What pre-parations have been made! All the old Blue Coat Pensioners of Jesus Hospital have been measured, fitted, and supplied with new blue coats and breeches for the Fair Sunday. Kitchens, barns, cellars, and out-houses have been lime washed. The Blue Bell, the Wool-Pack, the Sun, and the Crown Inns have scented the

whole town with new beer. Pigs have been
killed by the farmers, fat oxen by the butchers,
and tripe prepared by the dressers. All the
neighbouring fields have been hired weeks ago.
This is one of the most ancient fairs in the
county. Formerly, from the year 1154, a Sunday
market was held, but in 1204 the day was
changed to Monday, and by royal charter a fair
was granted to the town, commencing each year
on Trinity Sunday Eve, and lasting through the
five following days.

A great deal of beer will be drunk if the
weather is hot, and although Rowell has nine
or ten public-houses, yet there will not be
accommodation enough in the town. Green oak
boughs are therefore fixed above many a cottage
door to show that the inmate has a special right to
sell beer during the fair, and many a quarrel will
take place in these little "bough houses," as they
are called. Ostlers have the privilege of taking
in, on their own account, the farmers' horses,
providing they fix over the gateway or stable
door a wisp of hay.

All the preparations for the fair being complete,
the ceremony of proclaiming it takes place at
four o'clock on Saturday afternoon. The Squire's

Hill is alive with horses. Riding on a noble steed comes the Lord of the Manor, or if it is only his deputy, he sits on a common hack with mace in hand and the proclamation tied to his neck with blue ribbon. This officer is preceded by six or eight halberdiers, and followed by the Yeomanry Band on horseback. The lines of Macaulay apply well to the Rothwell procession as it nears the Market Hill :—

> " With his white hair unbonnetted the stout old sheriff comes,
>   Before him march the halberdiers, behind him sound the
>   drums ;
>   His yeomen round the market-cross make clear an ample
>   space,
>   For there behoves him to set up the Standard of Her Grace ; "
>   etc.

The proclamation (which is still read every year at the opening of the old charter fair early on Monday morning, instead of as formerly on the previous Saturday afternoon) would be read nearly as follows :—

" Whereas, heretofore, his late Majesty King James the First, and his progenitors, Lords of the Manor of Rothwell had, and used to have one fair in the year, to be holden in the said Manor, which said Manor is now by good and lawful means come to John Borlase Tibbits, Esq. He, the said John Borlase Tibbits, Esq., doth by these presents, notify and declare, that the said fair shall begin this **Monday** after the feast of the Holy Trinity, and so to continue for the space of five days next, after the holding and keeping of it, and no longer, during which time it shall be lawful for all her Majesty's subjects to come and to go, to buy and to sell all manner of cattle, merchandise, and other stuff being saleable ware and allowed to be bought and sold by the laws of this kingdom. No toll for cattle ; stakes for horses, sheep-pens, shows, and stalls are charged for as heretofore. And he further strictly chargeth and commandeth all persons within the liberties of the said fair to keep the Queen's peace in all things, upon such penalties as the laws and statutes of this kingdom are provided.

"God save the Queen and the Lord of the Manor."

And now the proclamation having been read in the horse fair just behind the oldest dissenting chapel in the Midlands, in the cattle fair on the Squire's Hill, in the streets of the town, and also in the Market Place where the pleasure fair is held ; every salesman shouts "God save the King," and commences business.

The number of visitors is very great. Farmers' wives come in on pillions, riding horseback behind their husbands. Market carts bring in numbers of tradesmen, and waggons carry crowds of country men, whilst the coaches are filled to excess.

Naseby, nine miles away, holds its own Rowell fair. The neighbouring town of Kettering also

104 BYGONE NORTHAMPTONSHIRE.

keeps up the anniversary, so that Trinity week becomes a great holiday time.

But the former glory and greatness even of Rowell fair are fast departing. No barricades are now required by the inhabitants to keep the herds of cattle from their houses and windows, —no "bough house" licenses are granted to the cottagers,—and although the fair is not now proclaimed until the Monday morning, it is practically all over by the Wednesday night.

Witches and Witchcraft.

By Eugene Teesdale.

SAYS H. P. Blavatsky: "Witch! mighty name, which in the past contained the promise of ignominious death; and in the present has but to be pronounced to raise a whirlwind of ridicule, a tornado of sarcasms! How is it then that there have always been men of intellect and learning who never thought that it would disgrace their reputation for learning, or lower their dignity, to publicly affirm the possibility of such a thing as a 'witch,' in the correct acceptation of the word."

In his "Sadducismus Triumphatus; or, a full and plain Evidence concerning Witches and Apparitions" (1726), the learned divine, Joseph Glanvil, Chaplain-in-Ordinary to King Charles II., and Fellow of the Royal Society, defined a witch as "one who can do, or seems to do, strange things, beyond the known power of art and ordinary nature, by virtue of a confederacy with evil spirits."

In 1678, Dr. Henry More, the Platonist, after
dealing with the derivation of the word from wit,
thus signifying in its origin a wise woman, goes
on to say, "use, questionless, had appropriated
the word to such a kind of skill and knowledge as
was out of the common road or extraordinary.
Nor did this peculiarity imply any unlawfulness.
But there was after a further restriction, in which
alone now-a-days the words witch and wizard are
used, and that is for one that has the knowledge
and skill of doing and telling things in an extraordinary way, and that in virtue of either an
express or implicit association or confederacy
with some bad spirits." And, in an account of the
"Arraignment, Conviction, and Execution of
certaine Witches at Northampton," printed in
London in 1612, we have yet another definition,
which is of value in that it "may at the least giue
notice and make knowne what manner of Persons
they be, of whom I am to speake. A Witch is
one that worketh by the Deuill, or by some
Deuillish or Curious Art, either hurting or heal-
ing, reuealing things secret, or foretelling things
to come, which the Deuill hath deuised to
entangle, and snare mens soules, withall, unto
damnation."

Having now obtained full and clear definitions of our subject it will be well to dwell briefly on the best means of finding out and defeating their evil aims. Reginald Scott, in "The Discoverie of Witchcraft" (1584), gives many directions. "To find out a witch : In die dominico sotulariæ juvenem axungia seu pinguedine porci, ut moris est, pro restauratione fieri perungunt : and when she is once come into the church, the witch can never get out, untill the searchers for hir expresse leave to depart." This superstition is named in a curious article we recently found in volume I. of "The Athenian Oracle" (London, 1706). At page 293 is mentioned the case of "a boy that was worn out even to a consumption by the common Load and Oppression of a Witch in the Night-time . . . an Elder Brother of his that came from the University, hearing the Relation of the Boy's Distemper, suppos'd the Reason of it, and ordered the Boy to lie with his Father, he himself designing to sleep in that Bed, and when Night came (according to my Friend's words) he Charm'd the Room, as is usual, to retain a Thief (for such things have been done, though we believe by no good means), and in the Night time he heard the Lid of the Chest under the

Window make a little Noise, as if a Cat or something else had leap'd out of the Window upon it, whereupon he rose and struck a light, and there stood an Old Woman, a Neighbour which he knew very well, in the midst of the Room; he bid her go, she answered, She could not 'till he dismiss'd her; whereupon he took her by the Hand and led her down the Stairs, and sent her home."

Reginald Scott tells us that "to be utterlie rid of the witch, and to hang hir up by the haire, you must prepare an image of the earth of a dead man to be baptized in another man's name, whereon the same, with a character, must be written; then must it be perfumed with a rotten bone, and then these psalmes read backward: Domine, Dominus noster, Dominus illuminatio mea, Domine exaudi orationem meam, Deus laudem meam ne tacueris: and then burie it, first in one place, and afterwards in another."

But many and various are the ways and means of detecting the "foul brood." These are briefly summarised by a writer in the *Retrospective Review*, 1822, and the list will give some idea of the ease with which an ignorant and credulous populace could condemn to torture and even death perfectly innocent and harmless persons. "Witches were detected," we learn, "by their inability to shed tears; by their not sinking when placed upon water with their hands and feet tied across, the right hand to the left foot, and the left hand to the right foot; by their mistaking, or omitting, when they attempted to repeat the Lord's Prayer; by insensible excrescences upon their body, supposed to be the Devil's marks; by an extra teat; by being watched till their familiar (in the shape of some animal, but distinguished from a real animal by the impossibility of catching or killing it) came for its daily meal of the witch's blood; by the testimony of the bewitched party; by the accusation of other witches; and by being made to walk incessantly till they were fatigued and bewildered into confession." In "The Athenian Oracle," already quoted from, the witch in reply to an enquiry "how she came to use such tricks," answered, "that a man came to her house, who relieved her, afterwards fetched blood of her, which she shewed, and there was a kind of Impression of Letters." Further we are told that she was induced to go to church regularly, but it was "a long time before they could teach her the Lord's

Prayer, and hinder her from stopping her ears."
Matthew Hopkins, the notorious witch finder,
had a variation of one of the tests given above,
which consisted in keeping the supposed witch
without food and sleep for twenty-four hours,
with her body placed in some uncomfortable and
fatiguing position. She was then closely watched
through a slit in the door to see if the familiar
came for his meal, and whether this occurred or
not, the result of the day's mental and physical
torture was a confused state of mind that generally
rewarded the efforts of Hopkins with success.

Northamptonshire has been the scene of many
a deed of witchcraft, and of many an execution of
witches consequent thereon. The attempt to
fasten a charge upon the Duchess of Bedford of
having by witchcraft obtained the love of Edward
IV. for her daughter, Queen Elizabeth, is a matter
of national history, and an important part
of county history. Travelling on to the year
1612, we have, in a pamphlet published in that
year, an account of "The arraignment, conviction,
and execution of certaine witches at Northampton, the 22 of Iuly, last past." After a
preamble and a dissertation on "What a Witch
is, and the Antiquity of Witchcraft" (from which

we have previously cited a definition) we are
introduced to Agnes Browne of Gilsborough,
"of poore parentage and poorer education, one
that as shee was borne to no good, was, for want
of grace, neuer in the way to receiue any,
euer noted to bee of an ill nature and
wicked disposition, spightfull and malitious, and
many yeeres before she died both hated and
feared among her neighbours." The chronicler
appears to have been himself somewhat
"spightfull and malitious," it may be through the
baneful influence of Agnes Browne and her
daughter Joan. This latter "Chicken of her
Dammes hatching" "was so well brought vp
vnder her mother's elbow, that shee hanged with
her for company vnder her mother's nose."
These two were accused of bewitching first
"Mistris" Belcher, and then her brother,
"Maister" Auery, by the infliction of dire and
grievous pains, as well as bewitching the body of
a child to death. "They stood stiffely vpon their
Innocence," but without avail. With these two
was executed Arthur Bill, "a wretched poore
man, both in state and mind," who was suspected
of bewitching a girl to death. Proof of his guilt
was short, when the ingenious justices and other

officers determined on the swimming experiment, in which they also included poor Arthur's father and mother, "that were both Witches." None of them sank, whereupon Arthur was arrested to stand trial for the tragedy. He, afraid that his father would bear witness against him, conspired with his mother, and between them the father was bewitched in such a manner he could not speak a word. Of this, however, he was relieved, and became by his evidence the chief cause of his son's condemnation. The mother, acting on the advice of her familiar, cut her throat to save herself from hanging.

Hellen Ienkinson, of Thrapston, and Mary Barber, of Stanwicke, bewitchers of cattle and men, also died at the same time. As the self-satisfied chronicler puts it :—" So without any confession or contrition, like birds of a feather, they all held and hanged together for company, at Abington gallows hard by Northampton, the two-and-twentieth day of July last past : Leaving behind them in prison many others tainted with the same corruption, who without much mercy and repentance are like to follow them in the same tract of Precedencie."

We have seen above some of the means of

detecting a witch, and reading through the pitiful story of the trials of the poor wretches executed in 1612, we find some of them followed. But let the tests fail, let all evidence be insufficient, it matters not ; the very pleading of innocence is jeered at as mere obduracy of a sinful heart, and in itself almost sufficient proof of the crime alleged.

A curious instance of witchcraft is given by Glanvil, in his "Sadducismus Triumphatus," as happening at Walton, near Daventry, in 1658. Widow Stiff's youngest daughter, "ten years of age, vomited in less than three days, three Gallons of Water to their great Admiration." Not satisfied with this she casts up large stones and coals, many of them too large to get into a man's mouth. Various other funny things happened about the same time, the bedclothes were thrown off the bed, the chests of drawers and other furniture so placed that it was almost impossible to move in the room, the Bible, which had been laid in one bed, witched away to another, and so on. Stones from some hidden and mysterious source were thrown at the windows which they broke, and as the narrator of this matter tells us that he saw the broken

H

windows, we must of course believe that they
were broken by witchcraft.   However, a suspected
witch was luckily sent to prison, with the result
that in a very short time the disturbances at
Widow Stiffs ceased.

In 1674, Ann Foster was arraigned and duly
found guilty of various evil acts.   She bewitched
a flock of thirty sheep, and set a house and barns
on fire with the aid of Satan her colleague.   All this
she confessed to, and was cast into Northampton
gaol, whence she was brought for trial to the
assizes, and condemned to be hanged, which
death she suffered on " the 22th of this Instant
August."

The fullest details of the compact with the
Devil, of the work of the familiars, and of the
pranks played by the witches, as well as of the
way in which evidence was obtained for their
prosecution, are given in two old tracts dealing
with the trial of Elinor Shaw, of Cotterstock, and
Mary Phillips, of Oundle.   These two women of
evil repute were a by-word in the mouths of their
neighbours, and to be revenged therefor entered
into agreement with the devil, pawning their souls
to him in return for certain powers of ill.   In the
course of nine months, "they had Kil'd by their

Inchantments and Witchcraft . . . 15 Children, eight Men, and six Women, tho' none was suspected of being Bewitch'd but those two Children and the Woman that they Dy'd for." In the same period, they also killed by witchcraft "40 Hoggs of several poor People, besides 100 Sheep, 18 Horses, and 30 Cows, even to the utter Ruin of several Families." Many "waggish tricks" are recorded of them, and much curious lore may be gleaned from the two tracts named which were reprinted about twenty-five years ago. These two women were condemned to a horrible death, "To be Hang'd till they are almost Dead, and then surrounded with Faggots, Pitch, and other Combustable matter, which being set on Fire, their Bodies are to be consumed to Ashes."

This appears to be the last execution for the crime in the county, or, indeed, in the country. Many cases of alleged witchcraft of a later date are recorded in various places, such as the *Northampton Mercury*, and as late as 1785 we read of the swimming test being applied. Still later, about 1810, we are informed by Mr. John Taylor, a similar trial took place at Butlen's Mill.

The City of Peterborough.

By Frederick Ross, f.r.h.s.

IN the fenlands of the Saxon Kingdom of Mercia, spreading south of the Wash, there lay, in the 7th century, between the Nen and the Welland, in the north-east angle of the present Northamptonshire, the small village of Mede-hampstead—the home in the meadows—surrounded by swamps, and inhabited by the rude Pagan Gyrvii or Fenmen. The Kingdom of Mercia comprehended the present counties of Northants, Lincoln, Huntingdon, Leicester, Nottingham, Derby, Warwick, Rutland, Oxford, Buckingham, Worcester, and part of Salop and Hereford.

The Kingdom of Mercia, at this period, was governed by Penda, a fierce old Pagan and bigotted worshipper of Woden, who made a vow to exterminate the nascent Christianity of the neighbouring Kingdom of Northumbria, and made raids into that country, slaying in battle King Eadwine, the patron of Paulinus, the Bishop of

York and Apostle of the north ; and, afterwards, Oswald, Saint and King, the second introducer of the worship of Christ, and, after a long life, was slain himself in a battle with Oswy of Northumbria, the founder of the Abbey of Streoneshalh, Whitby, which was the last battle in the struggle between the rival faiths.

Saxulf, a Mercian noble, who had become converted to Christianity, determined upon the erection of a Christian Church in Mercia, and fixed upon the village of Medehampstead as the site. Peada, son of Penda, who then occupied the throne, having become Christian, favoured his intention, and made a grant of an extensive tract of unreclaimed fenland for the support of the monks of the rising monastery. He died soon after, and was succeeded by his brother Wulfere, who seems to have maintained the old ancestral faith, as he put to death his two sons, Wulfade and Rufine, for embracing Christianity, Werbode, his steward, being their betrayer, who the monks tell us was strangled by the devil, a foolish proceeding on his part, thus to kill a useful servant. Wulfere soon after was stricken with remorse, confessed his crime, and vowed, by way of expiation, to be baptised in the Christian faith,

and establish Christian churches and monasteries throughout his dominions.

In the year 870, the monastery and church,
which were completed by Wulfere, his brother
Ethelred, and his two sisters, Kyneburgh and
Kyneswith, endowed with ample possessions
and privileges and dedicated to St. Peter, were
destroyed by the Danish Vikings, who sailed up
the Wash and plundered and burnt all the
monastic establishments of the Fenlands. This
occurred in the time of Hedda, 7th Abbot of
Medehampstead, who was slain along with the
whole of his monks.

Of this, the first monastery, Saxulf, the founder,
became the first abbot, and held the office until
the year 676, when he was nominated 7th Bishop
of Lichfield, at which place, St. Chad's Oratory,
it is presumed, the sons of Wulfere were converted, although the monks of Medehampstead
pretended that St. Chad's Oratory was within the
precincts of their monastery, planting a bay tree
on the spot, and surrounding it with cloisters
with nine windows of painted glass, wherein was
depicted with rhyming distiches, the whole story
of the martyrs, Wulfade and Rufine, which were
ruthlessly destroyed by the Puritans in the 17th

century. The most precious relic of this oldest monastery, was the right arm of Saint Oswald, the Northumbrian King, who was slain in a battle with the Mercian heathen, Penda, which remained for ages afterwards uncorrupted, and was the instrument, according to the monks, of a multitude of wonderful miracles.

The Abbey lay in ruin, with the monks all slain, and the land, which had been reclaimed from the swamp by the industry of the fraternity, in a state of desolation for a century, and the inhabitants of the village, which had gradually grown up round the monastery, and were in a great measure dependent upon it for employment, on the land, or in various handicrafts, or for alms, had been mostly dispersed, a few cottagers only remaining to gain a precarious livelihood from the ungenerous soil; when, in 970, King Eadgar commenced the re-edification of the church and domestic dwellings, which again became peopled by holy men. In this work he was assisted by Ethelwold, Bishop of Winchester, Dunstan, Archbishop of Canterbury, and Oswald, Archbishop of York, who came thither with a great company of nobles at the dedication, when, from the bestowal of great gifts and privileges by the

king, it came to be called Goldenburgh, but,
soon after, from its dedication to St. Peter, it
assumed its present name of Peterburgh.   It was
instituted of the order of St. Benedict, soon re-
sumed its former or greater dignity and
importance, and a town gradually gathered round
it again ; and was held in such reverence that all
visitors, even were they king, bishop, or abbot,
passed through the portals barefooted.   The first
abbot of the new establishment was Adulf,
chancellor to King Eadgar, who, on the death of
his son, came to Peterburgh, and, in the presence
of the king and his nobles, gave all his wealth to
the Abbey, and assumed the cowl, and, twenty
years after, was made Archbishop of York.   After
him came Kenulf and Elsin, the latter holding
the Abbey fifty years, both of whom were great
collectors of Saints' relics, of which the Abbey
became exceedingly rich.   Other famous abbots of
this period were St. Wolstan, afterwards Bishop
of Worcester ; Egelric, Bishop of Durham ; and
Leofric, a relative of Earl Leofric, the husband of
Godiva.

Brand was the last Saxon Abbot, who entered
upon his office in the same year (1066) that the
Norman William effected the conquest of England,

and he remained unmolested until 1069, in the midst of the turbulence occasioned by the Conqueror's subjugation of Northumbria, and the sturdy opposition of the Anglian and Danish population. In that year, Brand was deposed by William, and one Thorold, a Norman, substituted, who found his office anything but a bed of roses. Brand still maintained that he was the true abbot, and Thorold a foreign usurper, and was supported in his pretensions by the two famous heroes, Earl Waltheof, who was his nephew, and Hereward the Wake, "the last of the Saxons," in the Camp of Refuge in the neighbouring Isle of Ely, and the whole body of Saxons and Danes, calling to their assistance the Danes who were lying in their ships in the Humber, when they made an assault on Thorold's Abbey, which had been fortified by him in the shape of a castle manned by 140 soldiers. Enraged at the vigorous defence, Hereward fired some adjoining houses, and the church fell a prey to the flames. The monks were slaughtered, one sick monk in the infirmary alone escaping the fate of his brethren. The castle was pulled down 200 years afterwards, but the site, on a mound called Tout-hill, is still pointed out. The buildings were partially

restored, and the services continued until the year
1116, when they were totally consumed by a fire,
which broke out accidentally, although the monks
attributed it to a profane imprecation of the abbot
when the fire would not burn and he was impatient
for his supper.

Two years afterwards was laid the foundation
stone of the present Minster, and, in 1143, the
monks recommenced service in the choir, which
by this time was completed, but it was not until
1237 that the entire church was completed,
and consecrated by the Bishops of Lincoln and
Exeter. Although the church was finished in the
interior, other features have been added to the
exterior—the bell-tower, the western spires, the
lantern tower, recently re-constructed, the new
building at the east end, erroneously called the
Lady Chapel, all which have since been
added.

It was Abbot de Seez who called upon the devil
to blow up his fire, which he did so effectually as
to burn down the Abbey, but, however responsible
de Seez may have been in causing the destruction
of the building, we must admit that he applied his
architectural talent promptly and with unceasing
energy to the re-edification of the church, resolv-

PETERBOROUGH CATHEDRAL (THE WEST FRONT).

ing that it should compete in grandeur with its neighbours Lincoln and Ely.

Peterborough is considered the finest Norman church in England, Norwich only excepted, with features of Early English, as, for instance, the grand western front, without equal for massive dignity. As the nave was in course of erection, the style of architecture was in the state of transition from Norman to Early English, and presents a noble vista from the western transition end to the original Norman eastern choir. The original Norman tower appears to have become decayed, and was taken down, alarm being created by the fall of the Tower of Ely in 1321.

The second tower, for a long time in the present century, had presented suspicious evidences of instability, and, in 1882, it was determined to rebuild it, which has now been done. In taking down the walls, several interesting stones have been found of Saxon and Roman chisel-work, and the site of the original Saxon church, which appears to have been cruciform in shape. In the precincts was erected a chapel in the decorated style, in honour of St. Thomas à Becket, which attracted great numbers of pilgrims, enshrining, as it did, some paving stones

from the spot where he suffered martyrdom,
portions of his dress and drops of his blood, which
were brought by Benedict, a contemporary monk
of Canterbury, afterwards Abbot of Peterborough.
Benedict was the builder of the nave of the
church, and the finisher of the Chapel of St.
Thomas, whose life he wrote. He built, also, the
great gateway and the Chapel of St. Nicholas
over it. He was author of a chronicle—"De
vita et gestis Henrici II. et Ricardi I.," and a
work on "The Passion of St. Thomas," besides
transcribing the works of Justinian, Seneca,
Martial, and Terence, the Meditations of St.
Anselm, etc., and died in 1194.

Robert Lindsay, *temp.* John, is supposed, but
without absolute proof, to have been the builder
of the great west front, and to have glazed thirty
of the nave windows. Martin, a monk of
Ramsey, succeeded in 1226, who obtained from
the Pope the privilege of celebrating the Mass in
his Abbey, during interdicts, but in a low voice,
and without the ringing of bells. Walter of
Edmondsbury (1233) had to oppose a claim of
provisions with the Pope. Richard de London
(1273) was a great wrangler at law, the
"Chronicon Petroburgensis" being in great

measure filled with his lawsuits, which were
recorded by William Woodford, the presumed
author of the chronicle, and who succeeded to the
Abbacy.

Godfrey of Croyland, 1299-1321, was termed
the "Courtier Abbot," on account of his magnificence, luxury, and refinement of manners;
entertaining, on one occasion, the king and his
suite at a cost of £1,543 13s. 4d., which, including costly gifts to two cardinals and others,
swelled the amount to £3,646 4s. 3d. William
Genge, 1396, was the first mitred abbot; Robert
Kirton, 1496, the builder of the beautiful new
building at the east end of the church, and John
Chambers, 1528, the last abbot and first bishop.

In the year 1539, the lesser monasteries and
other religious houses, those with incomes of less
than £200 per annum revenue, were dissolved to
satisfy the rapacity of Henry VIII., his creature,
Cromwell, and the crowd of hungry courtiers,
who were eager to share in the spoil; and, soon
afterwards, the larger houses, including Peterborough shared the same fate, thousands of monks,
friars, and nuns being thrown destitute upon the
world, or pensioned with slender pittances. At
the first dissolution, when 375 convents were

dissolved, 10,000 persons were turned adrift from their homes with simply a donation of twenty shillings and a new gown, which, as Fuller observed, "needed to be of strong cloth to last till they got another."

Peterborough, however, fared better than the monasteries in general. King Henry proposed, as some sort of atonement, the erection of twenty-one new " Byshopprychys," to be endowed out of the confiscated revenues, and Peterborough, being one of these, Letters Patent were issued in 1542, constituting Peterborough the seat of the Diocese of Northampton and a city, the Abbey Church a Cathedral, and Abbot John Chambers the first Bishop.

There has been a series of twenty-seven bishops, some of them men of note, as William Lloyd and Thomas White, two of the bishops who were sent to the Tower by James II., afterwards deprived as nonjurors, White Kennett, the antiquary, Herbert Marsh, the controversialist, W. C. Magee, translated to the Archbishopric of York, and several to other Bishoprics. Among the Deans also, several were promoted to the episcopal bench—John Cosin, to Durham ; Charles Mannes Sutton, to Canterbury ; Simon Patric,

to Chichester and Ely ; Richard Kidder, to Bath
and Wells ; J. H. Monk, to Gloucester ; and
Thomas Turton, to Ely. From the Prebendaries
came John Williams, of Lincoln, and Dr. Bridge-
man, of Chester. John Pocklington, another
Prebendary, author of " Sunday no Sabbath,"
was stripped of his preferments.

Among the writers were Robert Swapham, a
chronicler of the Abbey, in the 12th century ;
Symon Gunton, Prebendary, 17th century, author
of " The History of the Church of Peterborough ;"
and William Woodford, in the 13th century,
presumed writer of the " Chronicon Petroburgensis."

Peterborough has the distinction of having
been the burial place of two queens—Katharine
of Arragon, who died at Kimbolton, Hunts.,
in 1536, and Mary, Queen of Scots, who
was beheaded, or rather murdered, at Fotheringhay, in Northamptonshire, in 1586-7, and
her head exposed, at one of the windows of the
castle, to the gaze of the multitude. They were
buried by the same sexton—Richard Scarlett,
who died in 1594, at the age of 98, and whose
figure is represented inside the cathedral, with
some verses beneath, in which it is recorded :

" He hath interd two Queenes within this place ;
And this towne's householders, in his life's space,
Twice over."

Very simple monuments were placed over their
graves, but the cathedral itself is said to be Queen
Katharine's monument, King Henry having, it is
represented, spared the Abbey Church, and converted it into a cathedral in her memory. The
body of Queen Mary was removed by her son,
King James, to Westminster Abbey.

There are fourteen monuments of bishops in
the church, and the graves of two Archbishops of
York—Elfricus and Kinsius, who had been monks
in the Abbey, and who repose there without
monuments.

Like all other ecclesiastical buildings, the
church suffered much damage at the hands of the
sixteenth century " Reformers," but still more
from the ignorant fanaticism of the Puritans of
the seventeenth, especially in the matter of
painted glass, of which Peterborough presented a
glorious display, which was smashed to fragments
by means of pikes, hammers, and axes, by the
soldiers and other zealots, with shouts of hilarity
and derision.

I

The English Founders of the Washington Family of America.

By Thomas Frost.

NO Northamptonshire family has received so much attention from the genealogists as that of Washington, and no places in the county have been so frequently visited by American tourists as the neighbouring villages of Sulgrave and Brington, where a branch of that family, from which the first President of the United States sprung, resided until past the middle of the seventeenth century. It has been somewhat difficult to disentangle the records of the family from the errors of the earlier genealogists; but it may be regarded as established by Mr. J. Penderel-Brodhurst (himself a member of a family connected by marriage with the American Washingtons) that the illustrious hero of the War of Independence was descended from the Laurence Washington whose tomb may be seen in the church at Great Brington at the present day. The first of the family mentioned by Baker, in his history of the county, was John Washington, of Whitfield, in Lancashire, whose great-grandson was Laurence Washington, who was Mayor of Northampton in 1532 and 1545, and one of the original trustees of the Free Grammar School of that town, named in the deed of foundation of Thomas Chipsey, in 1541. This Laurence received, on the dissolution of the monastic houses, a royal grant of the manor of Sulgrave and the lands of the Priories of St. Andrew, Northampton, Canon's Ashby, and Catesby. He is described as of Northampton and Gray's Inn, London, esquire, and is stated to have been a wealthy wool merchant. He married first Elizabeth, the widow of William Gough, of Northampton, who died childless, and secondly, Amee, daughter of Robert Pargiter, of Greatworth. He died in 1584.

The Manor House at Sulgrave, which is still in existence, though much altered since its erection, was probably built by Laurence Washington shortly after he came into possession of the estate. It is built of limestone, and consists of two stories, besides attics. The roof is chiefly of stone-slates, probably from quarries in the neighbouring parish

of Helmdon.   One of the chimneys of the north
wing is of stone, while the eastern group of three
is of old bricks.   The entrance hall remains, but
is now divided, forming a sitting-room and a
dairy.   It was entered from the front through a
porch, which is still standing, though the outer
entrance is now blocked up.   The Washington
arms, with the stars and bars sunk, instead of
being in relief, appear on the spandrils.   The
jambs of the wooden frame of the doorway from
the porch to the passage, on the west side of the
hall, have been removed, as also has the original
back-door, a new doorway having been made a
little more to the east.   The large window looking
towards the front has had its mullions removed.
The present east wall of the hall does not appear
to have been an outer wall, and it is stated that
the house originally extended about seventy feet
to the east of the present wall.   The wall on the
west side of the passage has no trace of a doorway
in it, and appears not to have been the original
wall, or there would have been doorways in it to
the kitchen and buttery.   The whole of the house
to the west of the passage, where these offices were,
or should have been, has either disappeared or was
never erected.   Against a portion of this wall and

part of the porch, piggeries have been built. A
portion of the original house appears to have
adjoined the hall on this side; and it is stated
that there was, at one time, a large arch, with a
porter's lodge over it, to the north-west of the
hall, which renders it probable that there was a
court on the north side of the hall. At present
there is, at right angles to the hall, a wing stretch-
ing about fifty feet northward, but this does not
appear to have been a portion of the original
building, as it is not in the right position with
regard to the hall, being too far westward, and
having in it none of the characteristic features of
the period when the house was erected. There
seems no reason why this wing should have been
erected where it is, as the kitchen, which forms a
portion of its ground plan, should have been in
the west wing.

In 1610, the manor of Sulgrave was sold by
Robert Washington, son and heir of Laurence,
and the family then removed to Brington. A
writer from whose description of the house some
of the foregoing particulars have been derived,
observes that, "as the house was arranged, and
at least *partly* built on a large scale, and as the
property and house were so soon sold after the

commencement of the building, it is not unlikely that the owner over-built himself, and so was compelled to sell.   There are other circumstances in the history of the family after the sale which point to this conclusion.   If this was the case, it is likely .that the house never was completed according to the original design ; and this again would account for the abnormal position of the north wing, and the absence of any vestige of a range on the west side of the court."

The Washington monument in Sulgrave Church, around which so much interest gathered in the course of the genealogical inquiry concerning the ancestry of the illustrious George Washington, was near the east end of the south aisle. A slab of grey Hornton stone bears a brass plate on which is engraved a headless figure of Laurence Washington, and the incision for his wife. Above this, in the centre, is a shield of the Washington arms, and below the fixture is the inscription.   Beneath this were groups of the children of Laurence, four sons and seven daughters, but these have disappeared within recent years, and must have been stolen. Of the six plates originally on the slab, that on which the figure of the wife was engraved, and the

portion of the companion plate bearing the head
of the husband, had been abstracted long before.
The plates are thinner than those usually found
on early monuments. The figure of Laurence
Washington is represented as wearing a long
loose coat, open in front, with hanging sleeves,
bordered with fur, under which he wears a frock
coat, buttoned up to the throat, and confined at
the waist by a girdle. The shoes are of the
broad-toed form of the period. The hands are in
the attitude of prayer. The inscription, in black
letter, is as follows :

"Here lyeth buried ye bodys of Laurence Wasshington Gent
and Amee his wyf by whome he had issue iij sons & vij
daughts wc Laurence Dyed ye   day of   anno 15
& Amee Deceassed the vj of October anno Dni 1564."

It would appear from the blanks in the inscription that Laurence Washington had the
monument placed in the church after the death
of his first wife, in 1564, and had spaces left for
the date of his own death to be engraven on,
which, for some unknown reason, was never done.
The figures of the four sons on the missing
brasses showed them as attired in frock coats,
knee breeches, and broad-toed shoes ; while those
of the daughters were represented in long gowns,

confined by girdles, and close-fitting caps.   There is no evidence, however, that either Laurence Washington or his wife were buried in Sulgrave Church.   In the course of some alterations at the church, a vault was found beneath the Washington slab, but this was shown by a coffin plate to be that of Lydia Jackson, who died in 1741.

The village of Brington, to which the Washington family removed after the sale of the Sulgrave property, stands upon an eminence, seven miles from Northampton.   The massive tower of the parish church crowns the hill at the entrance of the village from the side of Althorp Park, which lies in the valley below, and has been for three centuries and a half the seat of the Spencers.   The situation is a very pleasant one, with its long avenue of elms by which the church is approached from the high road, the fine old park below, and the wooded hill beyond, on which historic Holmby stands.   The picturesque old house of the Washingtons is situated in an outlying portion of the parish known as Little Brington, by which name it is distinguished from Great Brington, which is the full name of the village.   It is still in good preservation.   Above the door is the inscription :

"The Lord giveth and the Lord taketh away.
Blessed be the name of the Lord.
Constructa 1606."

The first, in point of time, of the tombs of the
Washingtons in Brington Church is in the
chancel, near the north chapel, and is protected
by a wooden flap, with a hinge, so that the slab
is never trodden upon, and, indeed, may easily be
missed by the curious visitor. Both the epitaph

SLAB ON THE WASHINGTON TOMB.

and the impaled arms of Washington and Butler
are deeply cut in the stone. The parish register
shows that Laurence Washington was buried on
the 15th of December, 1616, two days after the
date given in the epitaph as that of his death.
The following is the inscription :

"Here lieth the bodi of Lavrence Washington sonne and heire of Robert Washington of Soulgrave in the countie of Northampton esquier who married Margaret the eldest daughter of William Butler of Tees in the countie of Sussexe esquier who had issue by her 8 sonnes and 9 daughters which Lavrence deceased the 13 of December a. dni. 1616."

> "Those that by chance or choyce of this hast sight
> Know life to death resignes as daye to night
> But as the sunns returne revives the day
> So Christ shall us though turnde to dust and clay."

In the main aisle of the nave, about half-way towards the chancel, and therefore the first to attract the attention of strangers visiting the church, is another memorial of the Washingtons. Two brasses are set in a long stone slab, one at the head, and the other near the foot. The first bears the following inscription, very clearly and sharply engraved, and showing very little trace of wear, though it has been trodden by the feet of successive generations of worshippers for nearly two hundred and seventy years :

"Here lies interred ye body of Elizab. Washington widdowe who changed this life for immortalitie ye 19th of March 1622. As also ye body of Robert Washington Gent her late husband second sonne of Robert Washington of Solgrave in ye county of North. esqr. who depted this life ye 10th of March, 1622. After they lived lovingly together many years in this parish."

The lower brass, which is rather larger than

the one bearing the inscription, shows the arms of Washington, which, described in heraldric language, were *argent*, two bars *gules;* in chief three mullets of the second. In ordinary language, we should say, two red bars and three stars upon a silver ground. The workmen who engraved the brass, however, erroneously made the bars golden, instead of red.

Before leaving the old church at Brington, it may be noted that the parish register contains entries relating to the Washington family of anterior date to their occupation of a house in that parish. One of these records the baptism and burial of Gregory, a child of Laurence Washington, on the 16th of January, 1607; and another the marriage of Philip Curtis and Amy Washington, on the 8th of August, 1620. In the windows of Fawsley Church are six shields of arms connected with the Washington family, which have been a source of perplexity to antiquaries and genealogists, there being no known reason for their being there. There are two similar shields in the possession of Lady Hanmer, at Weston, and, as these are known to have come from the Manor House at Sulgrave, it is more than probable that those in Fawsley Church came from the same place. The first of these, in the order of time, is at Fawsley, and is charged with the Washington arms, below which appears "Wassh[ington]." The second is one of those at Weston, and bears the arms of Washington impaling those of Kitson, thus commemorating the marriage of John Washington and Mary Kitson. The third, also at Fawsley, has below the arms the names of Laurence Washington and Amee Pargiter, in the following form: "Wasshingtn and Pergiter." Fawsley Church also contains the fourth, with a similar presentation of the names of Robert Washington and Elizabeth Lighte. The fifth of the series is at Weston, and bears the names of Washington and Butler below the shield. The remaining three are all in Fawsley Church. The inscription on the sixth is almost obliterated, but is conjectured to have borne the names of Alban Wakelyn and Anne Washington, names which occur in the pedigree given by Baker. On the seventh the Washington arms impale those of Newce, a Hertfordshire family, but the place for the wife's name is blank, and no such marriage appears in the pedigree. The last shield of the series is so much mutilated that it can only be assigned to the place it occupies by the correspondence of the surrounding wreath and scroll.

Two of the sons of the large family of Laurence Washington attained the distinction of Knight-hood, and the eldest of these, Sir William Washington, repaired the fortunes of the family for a time by his marriage with the half-sister of George Villiers, Duke of Buckingham. How far the subsequent reverses of the family were due to the political and religious discords of the period cannot now be determined; but the Washingtons seem to have been unsettled for some years previous to that emigration to America which eventuated in placing the head of the family in the high position of chief magistrate of the young republic of the United States. From the fact that they were members of the Established Church it may be inferred that the social con-ditions of the latter years of the reign of Charles I., and those which immediately followed the fall of monarchy and episcopacy, were not conducive either to their material prosperity or their ease of mind.

There has been some contention as to whether the John and Laurence Washington who emigrated to America towards the end of the first decade of the second half of the seventeenth century were the sons of the Laurence Washington who died at Brington in 1616, or some other member of the family bearing the same baptismal names. According to the pedigree given by Baker, in his history of the county, the former view is correct, and it was for a long time generally accepted. Colonel Chester, writing in 1866, contended, however, that there was no evidence of the relationship, or even that they belonged to this county, and that there was strong presumptive evidence against the identity. According to him, it was only a coincidence that a John and Laurence Washington, of Brington, lived at the same time as another John and Laurence Washington, who emigrated to America.   Mr. Penderel-Brodhurst, while contending that "it is from Laurence Washington and Margaret Butler that the illustrious first President of the United States was descended," pronounces it "ascertained, after much research," that John Washington, great-grandfather of the American hero, and his brother Laurence were the sons of the Rev. Laurence Washington, rector of Putleigh, in Essex, but ejected from his living under the Commonwealth.   If this statement is correct, it would go far to explain the choice of Virginia for a new home, rather than one of the New England colonies of the Puritans.

As Dr. Draper remarks, in one of the introductory chapters of his history of the American Civil War, "The Royalist sentiments that had characterised the first settlers still predominated in the community, which was also firmly attached to the previous religious preferences of the mother country; for, though the Virginians had invited their Puritan neighbours in the north to leave their inclement abodes and settle in the more genial climate of Delaware Bay, they also resolved that no minister should be permitted to preach in Virginia, except in conformity with the Church of England. It was owing to this aristocratic tendency that, after the disasters to the Royalist cause and the execution of Charles I., so many of the ruined nobility and clergy found a refuge in Virginia." To that colony, therefore, John and Laurence Washington, whether they were the sons of Laurence Washington, of Brington, or of the Essex rector of that name, went out in 1657, or, according to Mr. Penderel-Brodhurst, in 1659, and settled on the banks of the Potomac,

in what is now the county of Westmoreland.

Shortly after settling down in Virginia, the wife
and two very young children of John Washington
died, and were buried on his own plantation.
He subsequently married Anne Brodhurst, the
daughter of a planter named Pope, who had
emigrated from England some years previously,
and whose name is perpetuated in Pope's Creek,
in Virginia. The lady had previously been the
wife of Walter Brodhurst, son of William
Brodhurst, of Lilleshall, in Shropshire. By his
union with her, John Washington became the
great-grandfather of George Washington, of
Mount Vernon, the first President of the United
States. That remarkable man was one of the
sons of Augustine Washington, who owned
extensive plantations in Virginia and Maryland,
which he divided at his death among his
sons.

There remains to be told of this remarkable
chapter of family history only the interesting fact
that the charges upon the Washington arms,
which George Washington had engraved upon a
ring which he wore, suggested the stars and
stripes of the American. flag. The arms of the

Washingtons of Sulgrave were, it will be remembered, two red bars and three red stars upon a silver ground. The bars became in the flag the stripes upon a white field, and the stars were multiplied in the upper quarter, next the staff, to a number corresponding to that of the States originally forming the Union.

K

Anne Bradstreet, the Earliest American Poetess.

TO Northamptonshire belongs the honour of giving birth to the first female poet who produced a volume of poetry in America. Her name was Mrs. Anne Bradstreet. She was born in the year 1612. The place of her birth is not absolutely certain. "There is little doubt," says Helen Campbell, the author of "Anne Bradstreet, and Her Time," "that it was at Northampton, England, the home of her father's family." At an early age she sailed with her father, Thomas Dudley, to Massachusetts Bay, he being one of the earliest settlers in New England. For some years he had been steward to the Earl of Lincoln. He was a man of means, and belonged to a good family, claiming kinship with the Dudleys and Sidneys of Penshurst. Literature had for him many charms ; he wrote poetry, and, says his daughter, he was a "magazine of history." He left his native country and braved the perils of

sea and land to settle in a distant clime where he
might worship God according to his conscience.
This stern, truth-speaking Puritan soon had his
sterling merits recognised, and held the governor-
ship of Massachusetts from 1634 to 1650. He
closed at the age of seventy-seven years a well-
spent life. After death, in his pocket were found
some of his recently written verses. His
daughter Anne was a woman of active and
refined mind, and had acquired considerable
culture at a time when educational accomplishments were possessed by few. She suffered
much from ill-health; in her girlhood she was
stricken with small-pox, and was also lame. Her
many trials cast a tinge of sadness over her life
and writings.

She grew up to be a winsome woman, gaining
esteem from the leading people of her adopted
country, and her fame as a writer of poetry
reached the land of her nativity.

She married, in 1629, Simon Bradstreet,
Secretary, and afterwards Governor, of the
Colony.

Her first volume was published at Boston in
1640, and was dedicated to her father. The title
is very long, and is as follows: " Several Poems,

compiled with great variety of wit and learning, full of delight, wherein especially is contained a Complete Discourse and Description of the Four Elements, Constitutions, Ages of Man, and Seasons of the Year; together with an exact Epitome of the Three First Monarchies, viz. : the Assyrian, Persian, and Grecian, and the Beginning of the Roman Commonwealth to the end of their last King; with divers other pleasant and serious Poems. By a Gentlewoman of New England." The book met with much favour, and soon passed into a second edition. In the third edition, issued in 1658, her character is thus sketched : "It is the work of a woman honoured and esteemed where she lives, for her gracious demeanour, her eminent parts, her pious con-versation, her courteous disposition, her exact diligence in her place, and discreet management of her family occasions ; and more so, these poems are the fruits of a few hours curtailed from her sleep, and other refreshments." The work was reprinted and published in London in 1650, with the high-sounding title of "The Tenth Muse, lately sprung up in America." Compared with much that was written in the age in which she lived, her poetry is entitled to à foremost rank, but it is not sufficiently good to gain for it a lasting place in literature. It mainly attracts attention in our time as being the first collection of poetry published in America.

Professor Charles F. Richardson, one of the soundest critical American authors, speaks of some of the poems as by "no means devoid of merit, though disfigured by a paucity of words and stiffness of style." The estimable writer of this volume won words of praise from her leading countrymen. President Rogers, of Harvard College, himself a poet, thus addressed her :

> " Madam, twice through the Muse's grove I walked
> Under your blissful bowres—
> Twice have I drunk the nectar of your lines."

All her critics were not so complimentary as President Rogers. Some did not think that a woman had a right to wield a poet's pen, and to such she adverts in the following lines :

> " I am obnoxious to each carping tongue
> Who says my hand a needle better fits,
> A poet's pen all scorn I should thus wrong,
> For such despite they cast on female wits :
> If what I do prove well, it won't advance ;
> They'll say it's stol'n, or else it was by chance."

Here are four lines on "The Vanity of all Worldly

Things," which, although short, is a favourable example of her poetic power :

> " As he said vanity, so vain say I,
> Oh vanity, O vain all under sky ;
> Where is man can say, lo ! I have found
> On brittle earth a consolation sound ? "

The next specimen of her poetry is an " Elegy on a Grandchild " :

> " Farewell, sweet babe, the pleasure of mine eye ;
> Farewell, fair flower, that for a space was lent,
> Then ta'en away into eternity.
> Blest babe, why should I once bewail thy fate,
> Or sigh the days so soon were terminate,
> Sith thou art settled in an everlasting state ?

> " By Nature trees do rot when they are grown,
> And plums and apples thoroughly ripe do fall,
> And corn and grass are in their season mown,
> And time brings down what is both strong and tall ;
> But plants new-set to be eradicate,
> And buds new-bloom to have so short a date,
> Is by His hand alone that nature guides, and fate."

The lines which follow were written in the prospect of death, and addressed to her husband :

> " How soon, my dear, death may my steps attend,
> How soon 't may be thy lot to lose thy friend,
> We both are ignorant.   Yet love bids me
> These farewell lines to recommend to thee,
> That, when that knot's untied that made us one
> I may seem thine, who in effect am none.

"And, if I see not half my days that's due,
What Nature would God grant to yours and you.
The many faults that well you know I have,
Let be interred in my oblivious grave;
If any virtue is in me,
Let that live freshly in my memory;
And when thou feel'st no griefs, as I no harms,
Yet live thy dead, who long lay in thine arms;
And, when thy loss shall be repaid with gains,
Look to my little babes, my dear remains,
And, if thou lov'st thyself or lovest me,
These, oh protect from step-dame's injury!
And, if chance to thine eyes doth bring this verse,
With some sighs honour my absent hearse,
And kiss this paper, for thy love's dear sake,
Who with salt tears this last farewell doth take."

In the year 1666, her house at Andover was consumed by fire, and her letters and papers destroyed, which put an end to one of her literary projects. Six years later she died, at the age of sixty years. Her loss was keenly felt by her many admirers. It is said of her by an American author: "Her numbers are seldom correct, and her ear had little of Milton's tenderness or Shakespeare's grace; yet she was the contemporary of England's greatest poets, the offspring of that age of melody which had begun with Spenser and Sidney, an echo, from the distant wilderness, of the period of universal

song." Several of her descendants are amongst
the most gifted of American poets ; they include
Channing, Dana, Holmes, and others.　Her
husband nearly reached the age of a hundred
years, and was termed "the Nestor of New
England."

Liber Custumarum, Villæ Norhamptoniæ.

By Christopher A. Markham, f.s.a.

THE first charter acquired by Northampton was granted in 1189 by Richard I., and thus the records belonging to the borough are both ancient and valuable. These are examined and scheduled by the Rev. C. H. Hartshorne, in his "Historical Memorials of Northampton;" but although he mentions all the grants, charters, and miscellaneous records, he does not notice the very interesting old Book of Customs still preserved amongst the borough archives.

This book contains 148 folios of fine vellum, the boards are of oak, covered with calf, on which various devices are stamped. At the corners and in the centre of each board are plates of brass, and the book is secured by brass clasps. The binding is of the beginning of the sixteenth century. The writing being of the fifteenth century, or perhaps earlier, it is beautifully clear, and almost the whole is written by one hand, the capitals being mostly rubricated.

On the five fly leaves, before the actual customs commence, are the following common forms :

Form for making Supersedeas, or staying the process of law ; this is written in Latin, and is directed to John Asteley, who was mayor of the town in the year 1488-89.

Form of a Power of Attorney, dated 1448, commencing, " I A.B. of Norhampton etc mchaunt of the staple at calles have made ordeiyned and substitute C.D. mchaunt of the same staple myn att°ney," and ending, " To all and singler the pmissz above wreton I have sette my seale etc and at the speciall Instance and request of me in so moche as my seale is un-knowen to many of you the worshippfull ssr. ff. B. mayre of the toun above seid hath sette the seall of his office the day and yere above seide etc."

Form of Release from the King, this is preceded by a request of the king's "trewe and feithfull liege men John Wattes and Thomas Bodyngton * late baillifz of your towne of Norhampton to graunte your gracious lettres of Prive Seall in forme as folowith to be made and

---

* They were bailiff; in the year 1487.

the seide late Bailliffz shall pray to God for preservacioun of your most noble and royall estate." King Henry then of his "speciall grace and mere mocion and for certain considerations him speally mevyng did pardon remite and relesse unto the seide John Wattes & Thomas Bodyngton" the moneys due from them after their year of office.

Letters Patent from the King concerning the Peace of the Town. These are directed " to his trustee and well beloved greeting them well and not doubting but that their wisdoms could remember and well consider that the use and encreasing of sad rule and good governance in every city and town first and principally pleaseth God establish perfect rest and tranquility noresheth and encreaseth love causeth plenty and laws to have their due causes justice to be indeferently ministered and executed and further directing them by their best wisdoms to see that good rule should be firmly had and effetually followed within their jurisdiction and they were to certify to the King the names of the offenders with the speciality of their offences and letting them witt that if it came to the King's ears and perfect knowledge that they suffered such misruled people he (the King) would so sharply lay it to their blame as should be a fearful precedent and grevous example to all other his subject." These letters were no doubt directed to the mayor and corporation of the town.

Letters Patent from the King to the Mayor respecting arrow makers: To "his welbeloved Symond Motte* gretyng" assigning to him the duty of arresting and taking all arrow makers as well within the liberty as without, and to take them to the King's works and put them in his wages in his City of London, "and the same arowes and tymber for the same arowe hedes silk wax ffethurs stuffures whatsoeve ther bee the which for the workes aforesaide shall be sene behoneable for our money in this ptie resonabley to be paied to take to arrest and to provide."

This ordinance brings to one's mind the time when England's defence consisted in the strong arm and steady eye of her yeomen; when each town had its arrow manufacturers, and each village its shooting ground, often still called by the name of the Butts.

And *Letters Patent from the King to the*

---

* Query was this the John Motte who was Mayor in 1527 and again in 1538.

Mayor respecting the Levying of Troops. After these fly leaves, the customs proper commence, being preceded by a table of the headings of the chapters. After the table are these words: " Usages and the Laws of the Town of Northton confermed bi the charters of diverse kynges of England by the purchases of old wise men of the same Town."

These customs occupy eighty chapters, and, as it is impossible to deal with them all, it is proposed to abstract some of the most interesting portions.

The first chapter deals with lands and tenements bought after the usage and customs of Northampton, and holden a year and a day.

The second chapter is headed " ffor to aske a cate of londe and in whiche maner :" the commencement is " Purveide hit is allso that if any man haue londes tenements or rents of his heritage or of purchase and he that lond tenement or rent nedith to sellyn his kyne allwey shall be moste next to ask the cate than any man ellis or the chefe lorde if there be no man of the lynage and if the chefe lorde take the sales be he forbarred of the cate."

This word " cate " is a contracted form of

the old French word "achate," meaning a
purchase.

By chapter four "if any man take a wife hit
shall be good to dowen his wyfe at his wylle in a
certeyne summe of siluer."

Chapter eight deals with a husband's right to
a life interest in his wife's lands after her death,
by courtesy, providing "that if any man take a
wyffe with free marriage and get a childe on her
and the crie of the childe be herde with inne
the hows after the deth of the wyfe he shall hold
that ffree marriage to the terme of his lyffe."

By chapter twelve it is also granted "that if
any man haue dwelled withouten chalenge of his
lorde in the town of Norhampton a yere and a
day and he be fyre house holdyng at loot and
scotte he shall dwelle free ther by the frannchise
of the towne."

In chapter eighteen it is provided "that if any
strange man that ledeth wolle into the town of
Norhampton may not sellen his wolle dept
yn but all hole to gedere And that no
strainge man may byen wolle in the town of
Norhampton but if it be in tyme of the feyre or
of good men of the same town And that no
strainger may byen threde in Norhampton for

to leden it out of the town but in tyme of a feire
No strainger ne may byen fressh hydes or pelts
in Norhampton but in tyme of ffeyr And that
no marchaunde of this shire no non other
strainger of other shires that comyth into
Norhampton with wolle hides talowe honey or
chese or fflesshe shall no where leyen down but
in the kynges shoppe And there to be purveide
a common shoppe."

By chapter nineteen "if any man have noryshed
tapster or servaunte and they of wikked wille
haue withdrawen or voyden her servise" the
bailiffe is to punish them.

Chapter twenty-two states that if a man "be
summoned" before the mayor and he "withsitt
the sommouns" he is to amerced at two shillings.
"And hit is to be undirstonden that a ryche man
be amercied at ijs. a mene man at xijd a poore
man at vjd And theise ameriaments be their
turned in to the profite of the commoune."

By chapter twenty-five no "ffysher nor
other man that fisshe sellith" is to buy fish of
any man bringing fish to the town before he
brings it into the market. And no merchant is
to go out of the town "nygh nor ffer by xxiiij.
myles from Norhampton for to byen ffysh or salte

for to derthen the towne." If he do so he is to be fined two shillings. And if he do so thrice "and thereof be overtaken fforswere he the craft a yere and a day."

Chapter twenty-six: All "baxsters" are to "setten in a serteyn stede togedyr and on on rowe allso as they do of Eckton* and all other strange Baxsters," and they are not to keep any bread at home to "derthern the chepying."

Chapter twenty-seven: No man "that bereth burthens of hay or of strawe pese strawe or bene strawe into towne ne come it nought doun to the erthe from his hedde tyll they have solde hit. And if their done lese they the burthene."

Chapter twenty-eight: Timber also is not to be laid "down to the kynges grounde" till it be sold.

Chapter thirty: No "huckster man nor woman of Norhampton ne gon owte of the town at non of the gates ne in no strete ne in other hydynges But in the kynges chepyng . . . to buy ffyshe nor hennes nor kokkes nor chese nor non other vitaile nor wode nor cole for to derthen the vitaile And no man ne bye suche

* A village about six miles from the town.

thyng beforn the prime be rungen at all holowen
chirche." *

Chapter thirty-five : If any man be "sommoned
to waken in the town that nede ben he shall sende
no man to wache for him But yf he nan ne
convenable and defensable And that wacche be
made from house to house so as it cometh a
bougte And that none be released nor forborn
but if he be a warkeman that lyveth uppon his
owne hondes."

Chapter thirty-eight : No man to take any
other man's servant, "but if it so be that he witte
howe and in what manere he be departed from
his maister that he served and that he be departed in good maner."

Chapter forty-one : If "any man or woman
ley his peny uppoun any marchandyze tille that
the seller hym hath granted the marchandise
leseth a peny to the profite of the bailliz and
good leve be to the other That wolle that
marchandize after byen And if any marchaund
bye be lasse than by a ferthyng hole but yf it be
peltis to parchmyn be in mercy of ye baillifs of
vjd."

Chapter forty-five : No "bocher" is to "haunte

* All Hallows, or as it is more commonly called, All Saints, is the
principal church still standing in the centre of the town.

L

the office of the bocherye as a maister " till he pay
3s. 4d. to the town " os they in olde tyme were
wonte to geven."

Chapter forty-seven : No butcher is to " sellen
sussemy flesshe fressh ne flesshe of a dede gote
ne calidiouns of a shepe nor Nete nor hedys of
calveren nor of Nete nor such manere of fowle
thynges but under the pillorie And if tho thynges
ben I foundene in other stedis for to sellen be
thei loste to the baillifz profite And the susmy
be geven to seke men of seynt Leorandis."

Chapter forty-nine : If " any chapman or
marchaund that marchaundoth with penyes of
straunge men " he shall be fined.

Chapter seventy-one : No one was to go about
the town after the bell of All Saints Church was
tolled at nine o'clock at night without a
light.

By chapter seventy-three, hardware sellers are
to sell their goods next the fish stalls in Mercers
Row.

The division into chapters continues only to
chapter eighty, after which the various ordinances
and customs are distinguished only by their
several titles.

One ordinance is to the effect that a miller

"shall have noo hoggys gese no dukkys at his mylle nor manere of pultre but iij henneys and a cokke."

An Innholder also is to sell "a pot of iij pyntes of the beste ale for jd."

A Taverner also is not to "make nor mdyll noo maner of wyne within his Tavern."

And a "Bere brewere" is to make "no maner of Bere but of good stuffe and that yt be holsom for mannys body."

In the thirty-seventh year of the reign of Henry "At the comon assemble holden at the guyhalde in the towne of Norhampton," Laurence Washington, the mayor, with the agreement of his brethren, the twenty-four co-burgesses, and the whole body of the town, ordained that whereas the bakers of the town had sent bread into the country on horseback every day, which was thought to be a dearthing of the corn that came into the market "from the vij daye of December next folowyng that no baker of this saide towne shall send forth of this towne into the country but one horse lodyd w^t breade any daye uppone the payne of eny default so taken to forfett brede and paye vjs. viijd. the one half thereof to the meyre for the tyme being and the other half to the vse and pfett of the chamber of the said towne."

This Laurence was Mayor of Northampton in 1533, and again in 1546, and died in 1584. He was possessed of Sulgrave, in the County of Northampton, and was the ancestor of George Washington, the first President of the United States.

Some of the punishments inflicted on various tradesmen for transgressing their assize are quaint. For instance, a miller was to have a quart of wheat given to him for grinding a bushel of wheat, and if he set it he was to have another quart, and he was not to water any man's corn to give him the worse for the better. And if he broke any of these conditions the fine was to be forty pence, and after two warnings he was to be judged to the pillory.

When a brewer buys a quarter of malt for two shillings he is to sell a gallon of beer for a half-penny, and to make forty-eight gallons of a quarter of malt, and so in proportion according to the price of malt. "And that he sett non ale asale tylle he have sent aftyr the ale Tasters to see that yt be good and abulle And that he selle a quarte of the beste ale within him for ob. (½d.)"

For continued neglect of these ordinances, he is "to be jugged to the cukkyng stole and aftir to the Pelorye."

If a fisher sell bad fish "he is to be jugged unto the stocks openly in the market place."

In this town, the stocks stood on the Market Square. In the year 1691, the town paid two shillings for removing these stocks; this was for the purpose of restoring or repairing them, as we find them in common use long after. In fact, entries occur in the sessions records of persons being committed to the stocks in Northampton in the present century.

The pillory also stood on the Market Square, although it does not seem to have been much used there at any time. In the year 1689, the following entry appears in the minutes of Quarter Sessions : "It is ordered that Thomas Smith of Kislingbury now Prison^r in their Mat^ies Gaole for this county being convict of counterfeiting a Pass under the hands of the right hono^ble Christopher Lord Viscount Hatton and Sir Roger Norwich Bart be continued in the Pillory in the Publick Markett place in the Towne of Northampton for the space of one hour betwixt the houres of twelve and two in the afternoon with a writeing on his Brest declaring his crime and be from thence re-conveyed to Prison there to remain till the next Quarter Sessions of the Peace to be held for this county and till this court shall otherwise order." Indeed within the memory of persons still living in Northampton, the pillory has been used as an instrument of punishment.

The following excerpt from the Sessions minute book appears to be the only case of any person having been ducked by order of Sessions. No doubt, this mode of punishment was generally ordered by mob law, and at once carried out, the cucking stool always being in a convenient place and ready for service, the people being at once jury, judge, and executioner :

"Trin. Sess. 23. Car. II. [1684]. That said ffranes Mason to be douckt in ye ducking stoole in ye towne of Northton Saturday next between ye houres of 11, 12, 1 and 2."

Doubtless this Frances Mason was a "communis rixatrix," though, being a widow, it is not easy to see why her scolding should offend; but the magistrates seemed to think it did, and therefore bound her over in the sum of twenty shillings to be of the good behaviour, and ordered her to be ducked at three different times on the next market day.

Thomas Britton, the Musical Small=Coal Man.

By E. E. Cohen.

THE traveller journeying from Northampton to Peterborough will, on his way thither, pass through the little town of Higham Ferrars—if he should care to break his journey—and possess both antiquarian and architectural tastes, he will find much to interest him in the old Church,—a charming specimen of decorated English architecture, an old Grammar School, and still more ancient Market Cross, the ruins of an old Castle, and Archbishop Chichley's School, that great Archbishop whose talents were recognised both by Henry IV. and Henry V. He was the founder of All Saints' College at Cambridge, and built, at his own expense, the Western Tower of Canterbury Cathedral. It is, however, of a more humble citizen of Higham Ferrars to whom I wish to direct attention. Thomas Britton, the musical small-coal man.

Was it not Henry Taylor who wrote "That the world knows nothing of its greatest men." Does it not frequently happen that even when accidentally it discovers a genius, it can learn but little of his earliest days.

So of Thomas Britton, we simply know that his parents were of humble circumstances, and that he was born in 1654. Who can say but the glorious example of his illustrious townsman turned his head towards the great city, and led him to think that he might also climb up the rugged spokes of fame's steep ladder.

Upon his arrival in London, Britton bound himself to a small-coal man, living in St. John's Street, Clerkenwell, close to the Jerusalem Gate, the man being so obscure and humble that tradition has not even handed down his name. At the termination of his apprenticeship, Thomas turned his face homewards; remaining at home until he had expended the small sum his patron had given him. Once more he turns towards London, and considering gratitude a surplus commodity in trade when one has to carve out a path for oneself, he set up a business on similar lines, in close proximity to his old master, who was still alive, transforming an old stable into a dwelling-house and store. Britton was naturally ambitious, and he became an ardent student in all intellectual pursuits.

Being also scientifically inclined, he commenced to dabble in—what the ignorant folk of his day considered the black art—chemistry. He constructed for himself a laboratory, which won for him much renown, and the character and scope of his experiments and researches drew from many a professional admirer, praise.

It was not only as a chemist he became renowned, but in the more entrancing art of music, for his skill both in the practice and theory was very great.

In his little rooms, for over fifty years, a musical club met, and here concerts were frequently held ; there can be no doubt it was the parent stem of the great London concerts. The guiding spirit of this musical club was Sir Roger L'Estrange, a celebrated literary man, and the censor of the Press of Charles II., the translator of Seneca and Cicero. Not only had Britton gained the regard of Sir Roger, but many other eminent personages were attracted to him by his deep love of literature, science, and art. His musical club drew together not only the men of quality, but many of the wits and savants of the day, who were only too pleased to honour him with their presence; and yet, whilst of lowly station, his unassuming qualities so commended him to men of the highest rank, that they always prefixed their addresses to him with Mr.

As he pursued his calling in his blue smock, carrying his small-coal in a sack, the populace would cry, as he passed down the street, " There goes the famous small-coal man who is a lover of learning, a musician, and a companion of gentlemen."

A writer of his day has left us this very graphic description of Britton's house and home: " On the ground floor was a repository for small-coal; over that was the concert-room, which was very long and narrow, and had the ceiling so low that tall men could but just stand right up in it. The stairs to this room were on the outside of the house, and could scarce be ascended without crawling. The house itself was very old, low built, and in every respect so mean as to seem only the fit habitation of a very poor man. Notwithstanding all these discomforts, this proverty-stricken home, this low hovel attracted to it as fashionable an audience as ever assembled at the opera." A noted belle and foremost lady of position in the land, the beautiful Duchess B——, was wont to remark, that "The pleasure in listening to Mr. Britton's concerts overwhelmed the sense of discomfort experienced in mounting his stairs."

Amongst the famous musicians taking part in these concerts we find no less a personage than Handel; Dr. Pepusch, the well-known composer of the overture to the "Beggar's Opera;" and Bannister, the famous fiddler, the first Englishman to distinguish himself on the violin. It was here that Dubourg as a child made his *debut.* So small was he that he had to stand upon a footstool so that the audience might catch a glimpse of him. Overcome by stage fright, the child nearly fell from his perch.

The subscription to the concerts was merely nominal, the charge being only ten shillings per annum. Out of that sum Britton furnished both the room and instruments. Coffee was handed round to the guests at one penny per cup. This was an innovation on Britton's original idea, which was to have had everything free. Those cooperating with him stated that no greater insult could have been offered than to desire to

remunerate him for services rendered. A song
writer, named Ward, the author of " The London
Spy," goes thus far in verse to confirm the
idea :

> " Upon Thursday repair
> To my palace, and there
> Hobble up stair by stair,
> But I pray ye take care
> That you break not your shins by a stumble ;
> And without e'er a souse
> Paid to me or my spouse,
> Sit still as a mouse
> At the top of the house,
> And there you shall hear how we fumble."

Britton's personal appearance may thus be
described : short and thick set, slightly below
medium height, with a straight open countenance.

There are two portraits of Britton still in existence, but of their present whereabouts I am
unable to say—both executed by his old friend
Wollaston. The painting of the first portrait was
entirely due to an accidental circumstance. It
happened thus :

One day whilst pursuing his ordinary round,
Britton found that owing to the briskness of trade
his load had become considerably lightened. He
was quite close to the home of his friend
Mr Wollaston, the painter, whose frequent invita-

tions he had never cared to accept, as he always had compunction in inflicting his society upon those who stood higher in the social scale. He further felt that his own calling was derogatory. With these impressions he decided to defer his visit. It so happened, however, that Mr Wollaston, who sat at his window in Warwick Square, spied Britton and called him in, Britton very timidly accepting the invitation. And this is how Wollaston came to paint him in his blue smock and his coal measure in hand.

Bateman's shop in Paternoster Row was the famous Saturday morning rendezvous of the connoisseurs, collectors, and bibliophiles of the day. It was no uncommon thing to see here the Duke of Devonshire, or the Earls of Pembroke, Oxford, or Sunderland, in animated conversation with Britton, who used to arrive upon the scene after finishing his rounds, attired in the old blue smock.

It was Britton's lot, like many another celebrity, to be misunderstood, and various motives were ascribed for his musical assemblies, which some folk were ready enough to assert were but the cover for seditious meetings, whilst the laboratory, as I have before said, left the impression upon the

vulgar mind that he had relations with the much-
maligned ruler of the lower regions, Pluto.

Personally he was styled in turn Atheist, Jesuit,
and Presbyterian. Despite all these dire calumnies
he was much respected, and won the esteem of all
who knew him.

Even the circumstances of his death are nearly
as remarkable as the episodes of his life. It was
due to the pranks of a ventriloquist, Honeyman by
name, a blacksmith by trade.

A friend of Britton's, Mr. Robe, a J.P. in
Clerkenwell, a frequent performer at the
assemblies, thought he would play a practical joke
on Britton, so he introduced Honeyman to the
house unawares. For the purposes of his joke he
arranged that he should, in sepulchral tones, which
were to appear as distant as possible, announce to
Britton his impending end, telling him at the same
time he might avert his doom by kneeling
down on the spot and repeating the Lord's
Prayer. Britton, in response to the voice, did as
he was bid. Returning home he took to his bed,
and in a few days died, leaving Mr. Robe, as a
legacy of his folly—the remembrance and remorse
following his practical joke. Britton was buried
in the parish churchyard on October 1st, 1714.

Britton left to his sorrowing widow a considerable library of books, an extensive collection of MS., music books and instruments, all of which were eventually dispersed under the hammer.

His character may best be summed up in the lines which John Hughes, the poet and dramatist, and the well-known contributor to the *Spectator* and *Tatler*, wrote under his portrait :

> "Tho' mean in rank, yet in thy humble cell
> Did gentle peace and hearts unpurchased dwell.
> Well pleased, Apollo thither led his train,
> And music warbled in her sweetest strain ;
> Cyllemis so, as fables tell, and Jove
> Came willing guests to poor Philemon's grove.
> Let useless pomp behold, and blush to find
> So low a station, such a liberal mind."

Another poet, none other than Matthew Prior, the poet, politician, and plenipotentiary of William III., likewise celebrated his fame in lines under his portrait, which run as follow :

> "Tho' doomed to small-coal, yet to arts allied,
> Rich without wealth, and famous without pride,
> Music's best patron, judge of books and men,
> Beloved and honoured by Apollo's train.
> In Greece, in Rome, sure never did appear
> So bright a genius in so dark a sphere ;
> More of the man had probably been saved
> Had Kneller painted and Virtu grav'd."

Old Scarlett, the Peterborough Sexton.

DEATH, that prime supporter of sextons, deals somewhat tenderly with them, frequently extending their term of life beyond the allotted threescore years and ten of holy writ, and even adding thereto the ten years of heaviness that usually close the drama of life.

Among the famous sextons thus indulged with special opportunities for the plying of their necessary business, Old Scarlett, the historic sexton of Peterborough Cathedral, occupies a distinguished position, his term of years being extended to ninety-eight. His death occurred on the 2nd of July, 1591, and he is reputed to have buried two generations of his fellow-townsmen.

When Catherine of Arragon, the divorced wife of King Henry VIII., died at Kimbolton Castle, A.D. 1536, old Scarlett prepared the grave of that unfortunate lady; and also performed the same melancholy service for another distinguished victim of Tudor craft and treachery, when the decollated corpse of the unfortunate Queen of Scots was conveyed from Fotheringhay Castle to receive its first interment in Peterborough Cathedral, A.D. 1587.

OLD SCARLETT.

Scarlett's epitaph alone would have served to perpetuate his fame, but the affixing of his portrait in the west end of the church has

M

intensified the interest in the old man and his
long years of work. The engraver's art has
introduced Scarlett's form and face into several
books, for the satisfaction of the curious antiquary,
and as a fitting accompaniment to his epitaph,
which runs as follows :

> " You see old Scarlett's picture stand on hie ;
> But at your feet here doth his body lye.
> His gravestone doth his age and death-time show,
> His office by heis token(s) you may know.
> Second to none for strength and sturdy limm,
> A scare-babe mighty voice, with visage grim ;
> He had inter'd two queenes within this place,
> And this townes householders in his life's space
> Twice over ; but at length his own time came,
> What he for others did, for him the same
> Was done.   No doubt his soule doth live for aye
> In heaven, though his body clad in clay."

In that interesting and cleverly conceived and
executed work, Dr. Robert Chambers's " Book of
Days," he thus refers to our notable Northamptonshire sexton : "And what a lively effigy—short,
stout, hardy, and self-complacent, perfectly
satisfied, and perhaps even proud of his pro-
fession, and content to be exhibited with all his
insignia about him. Two queens had passed
through his hands into that bed which gives a
lasting rest to queens and to peasants alike.   An

officer of Death, who had so long defied his
principal, could not but have made some impression on the minds of bishop, dean, prebends, and
other magnates of the cathedral, and hence, as
we may suppose, the erection of this lively
portraiture of the old man, which is believed to
have been only once renewed since it was first
put up. Dr. Dibdin, who last copied it, tells us
that 'Old Scarlett's jacket and trunk-hose are of
a brownish red, his stockings blue, his shoes
black, tied with blue ribbons, and the soles of his
feet red. The cap upon his head is red, and so
also is the ground of the coat armour.'"

Accounts of the Towcester Constables.

By John Nicholson.

ONLY an old account book, with its pages soiled and stained, torn and worn ; with an eloquence all its own, since the hand that penned the first pages has been cold and lifeless these two hundred years and more. Only an old account book, kept by parish constables from 1688 to 1727, from the bloodless Revolution to the coronation of George II., but full of interesting items bearing on the social and political life of our forefathers.

As we read such entries as the following :—

"1691. May 16,   Paid Robt Newman
            for mending and making up ye
            Holbeards -   -   -   -   - 13s. 0d.
            Pd. Richd. Wadge for Painting
            ye Halbd. -   -   -   -   -   6d.
    1717. Oct 23, ffor a New Watch staff   -   6s. 8d."

the measured tramp of our policeman on his beat gives place to the voice of the watchman crying, "Twelve o'clock, and a rainy night," and in mind

we can see him patroling the streets in his long
coat, with halberd in one hand and lantern in
the other; the light being a necessity to him,
as the streets were either ill-lighted or not
at all, and the roads were neither paved nor
macadamised.

There is no mention of coal in this book.
Wood seems to have been the common fuel.
Although coal was used, indeed St. Paul's was
erected by a tax on sea coal brought into London,
those great distributors, railway trains, were
unknown, and coal could not commonly be
obtained.

> "1688. Dessem ye 12, Pd ffor 6 Hundred
>   of wood -   -   -   -   - 4s. 6d.
>   13, Pd ffor 7 Hundred of wood   - 5s. 3d.
>   14, Pd ffor 3 Hundred of wood and
>   on pond of Candales -   -   - 2s. 7d.
>   22, Pd ffor 2 Hundred of wood ffor
>   ye woatch ye night after Betimes
>   ffier -   -   -   -   -   - 1s. 6d."

These are evidently special items, as there are
no others similar for such a quantity of wood
in so short a time; but there is no fuel except
wood mentioned, and no provision for artificial
light but candles, the price of which was fourpence
per pound.

One might suppose there had been a Ratepayers' Association in this parish, whose members
kept a keen eye on all parochial expenditure, for
in order to keep down expense we find entries
like this :—

> "1727. Oct 5, gave a big belyd Woman
> to get hur out of Towne   -   £0 os. 3d."

Poor woman! poor unborn babe! Then as now,
it was almost a crime to be poor; and she was
not the only one that received threepence "to go
away."

The succeeding entry shews how they coped
with outbreaks of fire :—

> "1688. May 10, To 2 Watchmen when
> Jno Bells chimney was on
> fier   -   -   -   -   -   1s. od.
> 1679. Aug 9, payed to 23 workemen
> at Mr Waples fier   -   -   £1   3s. od.
> payed for ale for the worke-
> men and other Labour and
> Watch   -   -   -   -   11s. 9d."

England was "merrie England" once upon a
time, so we find that on Easter Monday, 1696,
the constable spent 2s. at Joseph Kingston's,
"by order of ye Townsmen," and although we
are not informed for what purpose this money
was spent, it would probably be to provide

liquor or sports. Some people think a fair
or feast to be a very tame affair unless there
be a fight or quarrel of some kind, and an entry
under date 1699, Oct. 18, tells us that sixpence
was "spent on the Watch onn fair day night."

The following is curious :—

"1696. Oct ye 2, pd tto 2 men for Garding a
    Gipsee for shoating Benit sharpe - 6d."

Probably the "gipsee" would be in the stocks,
and those travelling tinkers, those peripatetic
pagans, have always been a thorn in the side
of our local constabulary.

The man mentioned in the subjoined extract,
evidently was so troublesome as to be a public
nuisance, and that parochial policy demanded his
removal :—

"1701. ffeb 16, pd for orders and Coppies of
    orders in Refferrence to remove
    William Hollan, and to send him
    away when the Townsmen shall
    please to give him notice Thereof - 3s. od."

The next extract, under the same date, gives
us an insight into bygone days and ways not
excelled by any other line in this museum of
local antiquities :—

"1701. ffeb 16, pd for ye Towne Plow £3 15s. od."

The modern Radical idea epitomised in "three acres and a cow" is but an echo of the days of old, when every householder was apportioned a share in the arable and pasture land of the village community. The allotments were divided into long, narrow strips, averaging about one-eighth of a mile in length, with *long furrows* from end to end, hence our word, *furlong*. The strips were separated by low banks, called *balks*, and the whole enclosed in a high bank, called *reins*.

The huge, heavy plough, drawn by four yoke of oxen, took so much turning, that it was driven as far as possible in a straight line. The ground was cultivated by co-operative labour, and the produce shared among the householders. One half lay fallow every alternate year, and formed common pasture for the village cattle, while the meadow-land was a distinct field, the hay of which was also distributed as fairly as the agricultural produce.

Scolding women were soused under water.

> "1688. Aug 24, Pd for the reppare ye
>   Cookin Sttool and all charges for
>   tto Duck Alis Gones in   -   - 19s. 6d."

Drunkards were laid by the heels, and had time

for reflection with their feet fast in the stocks, until they were sober.

"1702. June 4, pd for watching
     drunken woman in ye stocks £00 00 04."
"1689. April ye 29, Pd for watching 3
     in ye stocks   -   -   -   1s. 0d."

An old man told me that when a new pair of stocks had been erected in their village, they were watched for several nights by the constable and his friends, to prevent their removal or destruction by those to whom they were meant to be a terror. Lulled to a sense of false security by their non-molestation, the watch was removed, and next morning the stocks were gone. Diligent search discovered not their hiding-place, and the secret was so well kept that no clue could be obtained. A very dry summer, years afterwards, almost dried up the village pond, and there, in the middle, among mud and dead cats, were the long-lost stocks. Thus one is not very much surprised at an entry like this :—

"1694 (5). Mar 11, for warrant for
     them that brok the old
     stocks   -   -   -   -   £0 0s. 6d."

Therefore new stocks had to be "sette down," which cost 2s. 10d. ; and the timber for the stocks and "culloring" them cost £1 0s. 10d. more.

Both men and women were whipped, though their offence is not stated.

> "1688. Sep 29, To going to North-
> ampton wth Meakins wife
> and 7 more witnesses   -   2s.
> To bringing her back   -   1s.
> To 2 Watchmen 2 nights and
> days and Beere   -   -   4s.
> To whipping Meakins wife
> and a whip   -   -   -   1s. 2d.
> 1689. April ye 1, pd to keeping Henry
> Griffin   -   -   -   -   £0 0s. 6d.
> Pd for whipping him   -   £0 0s. 6d."

Having found herein the cucking-stool, the stocks, and the whipping-post, there yet remains the pillory, which was repaired in 1699, at a cost of 3s. ; and on

> "1727. Feby 9, Pd ye mans charge
> yt stud In ye Pereley   -   £0 4s. 6d."

In 1688, James II. deserted the throne, throwing the Great Seal into the Thames as he fled. Ireland remained loyal to him, under the Lord-Lieutenant Tyrconnel, who had 50,000 men in arms, and it shews how afraid the English were that this army would be used for invading England when inland counties felt the alarm.

> "1689. Jan 16, To Wm Hastings for 4lb of
> Candles when ye Alarm of the
> Irish was   -   -   -   -   1s. 4d.

"To James Thomas for 2 Links att
    The Marine - - - -   6d.
  To Robt Newman for Powder and
    Ball - - - - -   6d.
  19, To Bread for 200 soldiers - 7s. 4d.
  20, To bread for more soldiers - 3s. 6d."

These were the days of the press gang, when men deemed suitable for the Navy were seized and hurried off to serve as seamen, *nolens volens.*

"1693. Feb 16, pd 2 men for Gardine
    sum Imprest men - - £00 02 00
  Mar 28, ffor Carrying an
    Imprest man - - - 00 03 06."

To prevent such outrageous abduction, many men obtained and carried on their person a Protection Order, a copy of which is subjoined :—

"No. 40. J. Ferraby, Printer,
                                 Butchery, Hull.

These are to Certify whom it may concern, That the Bearer hereof,

James Spencer, aged 19 years, middle stature, fair complexion, wears his own light hair loose,

Is one of the Seventy Men employed by Messrs. Westerdell and Barnes, Shipwrights, at Hull, and entered in their Protection.
        Dated the Sixth day of October, 1787.
    (Signed)   T. WESTERDELL & BARNES."

But if the press gang were determined to have any particular man, even if he had an Order, they would not scruple to steal it, and then impress him for being without one.

Louis XIV. of France espoused the cause of the deposed James II., and collected a large army with which to invade England and dethrone his great rival, William III. The defeat of his fleet at La Hogue disconcerted his plans, and the Treaty of Ryswick was signed by William and Louis on the 20th of September, 1697. Shortly afterwards comes this notice in the book under our review :—

> " 1697. Oct ye 10. Spent in Proclaiming ye
> Peace - - - - - 2s. od.
> Oct ye 26. Spent at the Proclaim-
> ing Peace - - - - 3s. od."

Five years later the war of the Spanish Succession was undertaken to preserve the balance of power in Europe.

> " 1702. May 19, for proclaiming Warrs by
> orders - - - 2s. od.
> 29, Spent at Proclaiming of
> War - - - 2s. od."

George I. died on the 10th of June, 1727, and a few days afterwards George II. was proclaimed king. " The king is dead. Long live the king!"

"1727. June ye 20, Pd for Ribings to
    hang upon ye Constables
    Stafe, and outher Expences
    yt Day being ye Day of Pro-
    clamation of ye King   £2 5s. 6d."

In the autumn of the same year George II. was crowned.

"1727. Oct 11, Spent atte ye Crowne
    Ashan Day - - - - 2s. 0d.
    Oct 30, Spent at ye Crownation - 2s. 0d."

In three of the above extracts there are two items of different dates bearing on the same subject. This is owing to there being two constables, as a rule, for the same year, which ran from March to March. Here followeth a list of the constables, with their year of office :—

"1688. Robert Barratt and George Stokes.
1689. John Day, Thomas Wood, Will Wills (March to December).
1691. Thomas Summers.
1692. William Brett, Richard Marshall.
1693. Edward Butler.
1694. George Smith.
1695. George Carter, John Smith.
1696. Abraham Shackleton, John Goodchild.
1697. Richard Ratnitt, Richard James.
1698. Richard Watson, William Harris.
1699. Thomas Oldham.
1700. Lawrence Savage, Henry Perrin.
1701. Anthony Fletcher, William Peake.

" 1702. Samuel Orsborne, Samuel Carter.
  1703. Thos. Gillford, Edward Bloxham.
  1704. William Dimmock, William Marshall.
  1705. James Ffoddy.
  1706. William Shepard.
  1707. John Hall, Samuel Thompson.
  1708. ffarmar ffowkes, Lawrence Savage.
  1709. Thomas Cory, Henery Adkins.
  1711. John Capell, Abraham West.
  1712. Samuel Sharp, Thomas Newman.
  1717. Matthew Luck, John Pursell.
  1718. Matthew Luck, John Pursell.
  1723. Joseph Wilkins.
  1726. Thomas Carter, George Davis.
  1727. Samuel Osmond, William Goodchild."

In the above list of constables in only one case
do the constables hold office for two successive
years (1717-18); and in only one other instance
does the same name occur twice, viz., Lawrence
Savage (1700-8).

In the good old days they put a tax upon
heaven's daylight by taxing the windows of a
house. This window tax was imposed in 1695 to
defray the expense of recoining, and in making
up a deficiency in the silver coinage. It was
repealed in 1851, and the Inhabited House Duty
substituted.

> " 1717. June 18, for going to Northampton
>   wth the Duplicates of the Window
>   tax   -   -   -   -   -   2s. od."

The last item to which we shall call attention relates to the Poll-tax, which was abolished by William III., in 1689, but it is referred to in these accounts some years later.

"1697. Aug 11, for Returning a warrant
about ye Pole Tax   -   -   -   2s. 0d."

The Poll-tax was levied in 1380 for the defence of the realm, and the first imposition ranged from 4d. for a peasant to £6 13s. 4d. for an earl, but this was afterwards increased. The tax pressed very heavily on the poorer classes, and the rough way in which it was exacted greatly incensed the people. A brutal collector having offered a rude insult to the daughter of a tiler in Dartford, paid the penalty by his life. This was the signal for a great insurrection, for the whole country was in an excited state, and a spark was sufficient to kindle a great conflagration.

Wat Tyler's death at Smithfield, Richard's promises and pardons, which he was not allowed to fulfil, are matters of history. A large number of the rebels were executed, and the great rising came to an end, seeming to have only increased the load of suffering borne by our unhappy forefathers.

The Miserere Shoemaker of Wellingborough.

By T. Tindall Wildridge.

THE Church of All Saints and St. Luke, Wellingborough, contains examples of the Norman, Early English, Transitional Early English, Decorated, and Perpendicular styles of architecture. There is preserved in this building an unusually large proportion of ancient woodwork, the roof, the screen, and the stalls being all of great interest, as conservation rather than so-called restoration has been the principle upon which the guardians of the church have wisely acted. The stalls, six in number, and their miserere seats, point to the early dependence of the church upon the Abbey of Croyland, and to the officiation here, in some capacity, of a corresponding number of ecclesiastics. As is well known, the miserere shelves are secondary seats under the seats of the stalls, and though scarcely sufficiently wide to

afford a secure resting place, they were doubtless a great relief during the inordinately long
services which the capitulars had to undergo.
The name "miserere" is said to be from
these seats being raised at the chanting of the
51st Psalm, beginning *Miserere Mei;* their more
correct name was "Misericorde"—a mercy or
relief. They are also called "subsellæ" from

THE MISERERE SHOEMAKER, WELLINGBOROUGH.

their situation. One of these misereres at
Wellingborough is of special interest, as it is
evidence of a continuity in the staple manufacture
of the town from at the latest the reign of
Edward IV. This miserere is known as "the
Shoemaker." It represents a workman sat with
a board upon his knee, upon which are spread the
implements of his craft, among which can be
clearly distinguished the awl, "clincher" (a sort

N

of chisel), hammer, seat-file, and several cutting
knives.

He wears a costume very nearly approaching
the fashionable attire of the early part
of Edward IV.'s reign; his shoulders are
padded with the bulky waddings called
mahoitres, and his doublet and sleeves have
the appearance of being quilted or stuffed. He
does not, however, wear the long-toed shoes of
the upper class, for, supposing him a shoemaker,
he would have need to bear in mind the ordinance
by which any shoemaker or cobbler making
poulaines, or long-pointed shoes, for unprivileged
persons was liable not only to the forfeiture of
twenty shillings for each offence, but also the " pain
of cursing " by the clergy. The worker is shewn
holding a knife, evidently keen, with both hands,
and carefully cutting not a shoe, but a rose for
the decoration of one, while in the bosom
of his doublet he wears a smaller similar
rose. The whole action of the figure and the
minutely carved tools are undoubtedly those of a
leather worker, and it may be safely inferred that
he carving is a semi-satirical caricature upon the
costume of the day and upon the legal strictures
on dress; as also upon the wholesale decoration

of the adherents of Edward with the badges of the sun and the rose. It is but to "shoe the goose" to attempt explanation of all the fanciful designs of misereres, but it almost seems as though this mediæval humourist wished to say by his carving, " Nowadays all men dress as richly as the law will let them, and as for York roses, why even the shoemakers have to spend their time making them, and they themselves, forsooth, shall be decorated therewith." At either side of the shoemaker is an eagle seated upon a conventional bush.

Sir Thomas Tresham and his Buildings.

By John T. Page.

"BLESSED is the man," said Lord Brougham, "who has a hobby." To this trite assertion might well be added a benediction on the man who, having a hobby, also possesses the means wherewith to carry it out. Some hobbies are very expensive, and many a man has been forced to lay his hobby down with a sigh because he lacked the wherewithal to proceed further with it. Notwithstanding this, good work has often been done in the pursuit of a hobby, and it would be comparatively easy to adduce many examples in support of this statement. In the case of Sir Thomas Tresham, we have a man whose hobby was building, and although the times were evil for him he left behind much work that was beautiful and curious in design, and lasting in point of workmanship.

The grandfather of Sir Thomas Tresham, the

builder, was the first, and also the last, Prior of
the Order of St. John of Jerusalem, which was
resuscitated in the reign of Queen Mary. Notwithstanding this, he married twice, and several children
were born to him. His eldest son, having married,
died on the same day as his wife, leaving an
infant son named Thomas, two and a half years
old. In 1559, Sir Thomas, the Prior, died, leaving
his estates to his grandson, who was then fifteen
years of age. For some unexplained reason, this
youth, who was brought up by his grandfather, had
been educated as a Protestant. Henceforth his
history is a blank until we find his name amongst
those who received the honour of knighthood
from Queen Elizabeth, on the occasion of her
celebrated visit to Kenilworth, in July, 1575. By
this time he was also a married man and a father.
At the age of thirty-seven, in the year 1580, he was
converted to Roman Catholicism under the
influence of the missionary priests Campion and
Parsons. His life now became one long series of
fines and imprisonments. Before the year of his
conversion was out he was in durance vile, and for
the next ten years he spent a great portion of his
time under restraint, either in the Fleet, at
Hoggesdon (Hoxton), at Ely, or at Banbury. In a

letter written in 1593 he himself refers to the fact
that he had not been allowed to visit Northamptonshire for the past eight years ; but from this time
until 1595 he resided in the county in the bosom
of his family.   In 1595, he was again carried away,
and, except at a few brief intervals, he did not
enjoy freedom until within a couple of years or
so of the death of Elizabeth.

On March 25th, 1603, he played a conspicuous
part by proclaiming James I. King at Northampton.   James had secretly encouraged the
Romanists for some time previously, and this
made them very anxious to see him securely
seated on the throne.

The few remaining years of Tresham's life were
spent in peace and quietness in Northamptonshire,
and there is every reason for supposing that he
knew nothing of the contemplated Gunpowder Plot,
in which his son Francis was so deeply involved.

On September 11th, 1605, a little less than
three months before his son divulged the Plot, he
peaceably breathed his last.

Having briefly reviewed the eventful life of Sir
Thomas Tresham, we now turn to a cursory
examination of the remains of his handiwork in
the buildings which he erected.

The first of these structures is the Market House at Rothwell. Although the inscription of the year of its erection and the building itself were both left unfinished, an agreement in existence concerning "certain buildings at Rothwell Cross 2 July 1578" fixes the date accurately enough. It has been said that "if finished with

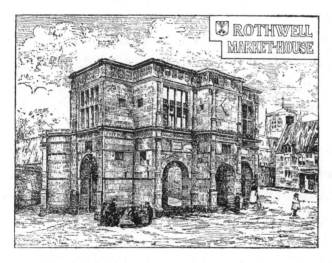

ROTHWELL MARKET-HOUSE

the gables and the finials, which it was undoubtedly meant to have, it would be one of the most picturesque buildings of its time." It is raised on arches and is square in shape, with projections at intervals, enriched with pilasters. Around the cornice are depicted the arms of various noblemen and gentlemen of the county, and around the frieze is sculptured the following :

"THOME TRESAMI MILITIS FVIT HOC OPUS IN GRATIAM DULCIS PATRIÆ FECIT SVÆ TRIBVSQUE NORTHAMPTONIÆ VEL MAXIME HVJVSQUE VICINI SIBI PAGI COMMUNE QUÆSIVAT NIHIL PRÆTER DECUS PERENNE AMICORUM TERPRETATOR DIGNUS HAVD TANTO EST BONO Aº DOMINI MILLESIMO QUINGENTESIMO SEP————."

From 1593 to 1595, Tresham was hard at work with his building. During this period he enlarged Rushton Hall, the family residence, constructed the curious Triangular Lodge at Rushton, and commenced the New Building at Lyveden. Several of the gables at Rushton Hall bear his coat of arms and the date 1595. It was here, during the progress of some repairs, in 1832, that a bundle of books and papers which once belonged to Sir Thomas were discovered in a cavity over one of the doorways. A quotation from one of these papers will very aptly precede our notice of the Triangular Lodge and Lyveden Building, and to some extent account for the introduction of the mystic element in their construction. It is contained in a letter written by Sir Thomas, presumably from Wisbech Castle, about the year 1584, and runs as follows :

"If it be demanded why I labour so much in the Trinity and Passion of Christ to depaint in this chamber, this is the principal instance thereof: That at my last being hither committed, and I usually having my servants here allowed me, to read nightly an hour to me after supper, it fortuned that Fulcis, my then servant, reading in the *Christian Resolution*, in the Treatise of *Proof that there is a God, etc.*, there was upon a wainscot table at that instant three loud knocks (as if it had been with an iron hammer) given; to the great amazing of me and my two servants, Fulcis and Nilkton."

The Triangular Lodge undoubtedly symbolises the Trinity. It has three floors and three sides. Each side is thirty-three feet three inches long, contains three windows, and is surmounted by three gables, each of which finishes with a trefoil on its pinnacle. The various shields, devices and figures which are to be seen on the walls would take too long to describe fully here, if only from their great number. Reference, however, must be made to the Latin inscriptions, which are very curious. In the case of the longer ones, which run round the walls just beneath the gables, it will be observed that, containing thirty-three letters each, they are strangely in keeping with the character of the place :

North Side.
" QVIS SEPARABIT NOS A CHARITATE CHRISTI."
South-East Side.
"APERIATVR TERRA & GERMINET SALVATOREM."
South-West Side.
"CONSIDERAVI OPERA TVA DOMINE ET EXPAVI."

Several shorter sentences are inscribed on different parts of the walls.

In the second storey on the south-east side is the doorway, which is approached by a flight of steps; on the same side, below the windows, are the initials T. T., and the date 1593.

At Lyveden there are two buildings known as the "Old Build" and the "New Build" respectively.

The "Old Build" is supposed to be the work of Sir Thomas Tresham, because the style is Elizabethan, but beyond that and the character of the workmanship there is no direct proof. The construction of the building betrays no signs of eccentricity, and has readily lent itself in these later times to the uses of a convenient farm-house. The "New Build" stands in a fine position on high ground surrounded by woods. It is constructed in the form of a Greek Cross, and is intended as a symbol of the Passion of Christ. On the key-stones of the arches are the arms of Sir Thomas Tresham and his wife, who was a daughter of Sir Robert Throckmorton. Each limb of the cross terminates with a large and deep oriel window. The interior of the building is now in a very dismantled state, and affords an easy vantage ground for all sorts of wild plants. Although it was never finished, it was not left in its present state of incompleteness. During the Civil War it received much harm from the hands of a certain Major Butler, who caused the timber to be sawed out of the walls for building purposes of his own, hard by at Oundle. Thanks, however, to good workmanship and strong cement, the removal of the stonework proved too great a task for this redoubtable Iconoclast.

Like the Triangular Lodge, this building is also covered with many devices, figures, and inscriptions. Various emblems of the Crucifixion, such as the cross, ladder, hammer, nails, spear, etc., are carved in roundels all along the walls above the second storey. Round the upper storey were carved the following sentences, but they are now sadly defaced and ruined :

" JESVS MVNDI SALVS +
GAVDE MATER VIRGO MARIA +
VERBUM AVTEM CRVCIS PEREVNTIBUS QVIDEM STVLTITIA EST +
JESV BEATVS VENTER QVI TE PORTAVIT +
MARIA MATER VIRGO SPONSA INVPTA +
BENEDIXIT TIBI DEVS IN ÆTERNVM MARIA +
MIHI AVTEM ABSIT GLORIARI NISI IN CRVCE DOMINI NOSTRI +."

The lower storey contains many shields for arms, but most of these are left in a very unfinished state.

The good workmanship of these buildings has before been alluded to, and it is doubtless owing to this, and to the durability of the Weldon stone, of which they are all composed, that they are in such comparatively good condition after having stood the storm and stress of nearly 300 years.

As we take leave of this subject we cannot do better than call to mind the quaint and brief sentence used by Fuller, who thus sums up the character of Sir Thomas Tresham the builder :—

"Hard to say whether greater his delight or skill in buildings, though more forward in beginning than fortunate in finishing his fabrics."

Northamptonshire Folk=Lore.

By John Nicholson.

IT is perhaps fitting that much of what relates
of folk-lore should be published under the
title "Bygone." Though stories of fairies and
hell-hounds, or of "Jinn with the burnt tail," may
still enchain attentive ears round the glowing fire
in the gloaming, these stories are but memories,
the world about which they tell has long since
ceased to be real, even to the mass of our rural
population, and now exists only in lay and
legend. How many of us have ever seen a may-
pole, except as a revival, not a survival; and few,
if any of us, even though gifted with the super-
natural powers possessed by the seventh child of
a seventh child, have ever beheld the tiny forms
of Queen Mab's followers sporting on the fairy
ring.

Schoolmasters and locomotive engine-drivers
have done much to level society, and banish old
beliefs and curious local customs; the one by ·dis-

semination of knowledge of books, the other by affording cheap and rapid transit to distant places.

Very old people have heard, and declare unto us, that it used to be the custom for a housewife, before retiring to rest, to carefully sweep the ashes and embers of the wood fire into a heap on the broad hearthstone, in the wide chimney open to the starry sky. On this warm clean stone she placed a basin or bowl of water for the fairies' bath, and if any of the family awoke during the night they might hear the tiny footsteps of the elves as they frisked over the cooling stone. These visits always brought good luck to the house, unless an attempt was made to watch the sprites, when they immediately sought fresh quarters, and tradition says that the watcher, from Peeping Tom downwards, always became blind.

These midnight marauders kept not the eighth commandment always, they seemed to think that the property of mortals was placed at their disposal, and robbed their enemies to enrich their friends. It is said that a certain farmer lost very many sheaves from his barn, for in these old world stories, the *barn* was the place where was stored what the earth did *bear*; we never hear of stacks in fairy tales. The thief or thieves could

not be discovered, though watch, strict and constant, was kept; until, one night, the farmer hid
himself among the sheaves to act as his own
detective. At midnight, two tiny elves came
tumbling through the pike-hole, and set to work
diligently making little bundles suitable for carrying away. At length, after much labour, they
paused, and one said to the other, "I twit
(sweat), do you twit?" "I'll twit ye, if ye bin't
off," said the farmer, as he rushed out of his
hiding-place; but the elves had vanished, and
never again annoyed that farmer with their
thievish tricks.

A South Northamptonshire legend tells of a
young fellow who was fortunate enough, one moon-
light night, to witness the revels of the fairy folk.
It is only fair, alike to both parties, to state that
the rustic was returning from a village feast, and
that says much for his condition, but, any-
how, he saw "a vast o' fairy folk" playing football.
Mortal though he was, he joined the throng of
tussling mites, and at length succeeded in kicking
their ball. It burst with a loud noise, the scene
vanished, and he fell to the ground stunned.
When he recovered he thought it had been a
dream but for the remains of the "bursten ball,"

and the presence of many golden coins, with which the ball had evidently been stuffed.

Many of the gods of our Norse and Saxon forefathers, when they were dethroned from their thrones of honour, still retained their power, and are now a power for evil instead of good. The gods became devils, bogies, or ghosts : and often perform wonderful feats of strength to thwart the designs of man. Hence we have a legend respecting Ninechurches, near Daventry. Its name at one time was simply Stowe, and here the lord of the manor determined to build a church upon a site duly chosen. Plans were made, and foundations laid, but, next morning, all the results of their labour had vanished. After a long search, the stones, tools, etc., were discovered some distance away, on the spot where the church now stands. Of what use is it being a lord of the manor if you cannot have your own church where you choose ? So everything was taken back, a second start made, only to be carried away during the night. Nine times did my lord endeavour to carry out his scheme, and nine times was he checked by the removal, during the night, of what his men built during the day. Finally it was borne in upon him that even lords of the manor have to give in, and the church was erected on the site selected by the unseen power. In order to determine who or what was the cause of the mischief a workman did watch all one night, but the only information gained was, that it was "summet bigger nor a hog."

Another story commonly related throughout Northamptonshire is as follows :—"A spirit asserted a claim to a field hitherto possessed by a farmer, and, after much disputing, they came to an arrangement by agreeing to divide its produce between them. At seedtime, the farmer asked the Bogie what part of the crop he will take, "tops or bottoms." "Bottoms," said the Bogie, who is outwitted by the farmer sowing wheat. The farmer thus secured the grain, stubble falling to the lot of the sprite. Next year, the Bogie chose "tops," whereupon the crafty farmer raised a crop of turnips, Bogie again coming off second best. Tired of this unprofitable farming, the Bogie agreed to hazard his claims on a mowing match—the disputed field being the stake played for. Before the day of meeting, the farmer stuck iron bars among the grass to be mown by his opponent ; and when the trial did commence, the unsuspecting goblin found his progress retarded

O

by his scythe coming into contact with these bars, which he thought were some hard species of dock. "Mortal hard docks these!" said he. "Nation hard docks!" His blunted blade soon brought him to a standstill, and as he could not sharpen unless the farmer also did, he cried out in despair, "When d'ye wiffle waffle (whet), mate?" "Waffle!" said the farmer, "oh, about noon, mebby!" "Then," said the disheartened Bogie, "I've lost my land!" So saying, he disappeared, and the farmer ever afterwards held undisputed ownership.

Witches and their reputed power must needs be mentioned in Folk-Lore. In Northampton, tradition says anyone could become a witch by sitting on the hob of the hearth, and after carefully cleaning and paring her nails, to give utterance to these words—"I wish I was as far from God as my nails are from dirt;" and there and then she was endowed with those wonderful powers which placed at her mercy all who incurred her displeasure, and which enabled her to change herself into other shapes, chiefly animal, but if wounded or maimed in that state, her human shape shewed the same injury. A woodman working in the forest had his food stolen by a cat, day after day, and after lying in wait for the four-footed thief, succeeded in cutting off a fore paw. When he got home he found his wife with only one hand.

A few years ago, there was a tree standing near the village of Tyresham, about which the following story is told. A man, with his little boy, was passing by the tree, when the little fellow begged for a stick from it, to play with. The man took his out knife and began to cut, but at once desisted, for a stream of blood spouted out of the cut made by the knife. A certain woman of the village, long suspected as a witch, appeared with her arm bound up, and was thus proved to be as suspected. Being subjected to the water ordeal, she ended her days in a neighbouring horsepond.

Natural perforated pebbles, horseshoes, and straws or knives crossed on the floor are believed to be efficacious preventatives.

The following word charm is used to prevent a thorn from festering :—

> "Our Saviour was of virgin born,
> His head was crowned with a crown of thorn ;
> It never cankered nor festered at all ;
> And I hope in Christ Jesus this never shaull."

For a mouse to run over a person is considered a sign of death, or the apparition of a white one running across the floor of the room.   To meet a shrew-mouse is ominous of evil.

The crowing of a hen foretells evil, but it generally falls on the fowl, for she is decapitated as soon as captured.   If the cock comes strutting up to the door, and crows on the threshold, a stranger may be expected.   A hen is always "set" with an odd number of eggs, to ensure good luck; and to further secure this desirable fortune each egg is marked with a small black cross.

For the cure of fever, and for stopping or preventing bleeding at the nose, a toad must be killed by transfixing it with some sharp pointed instrument, after which it is enclosed in a little bag and hung round the neck.

Among omens of misfortune or bad luck may be mentioned—to see a crow flying alone; swallows or jackdaws flying down a chimney; the chattering of magpies; and the desertion of a hearth by crickets.

If an apple tree bear, at the same time, both blossom and fruit, it betokens death to some of the owner's family ; while the discovery of a double nut augurs well for the finder.   In decorating the house with evergreens at Christmas, care must be taken not to let ivy be used alone, or even in profusion, as it is a plant of bad omen, and will prove injurious.

In making bread, the dough is crossed in order to make it rise quicker. If a person wash in the same water in which another person has washed, they two will quarrel ere the day is out, unless the water be crossed, by making the form of the cross with the finger on the water.

If a horse get a nail in its foot, it must be kept bright after it is taken out, or the horse will not recover from his lameness.

The hair cut off the head must be burnt, for if it be thrown away, some bird will probably use it for nest-making, and the original owner will be seized with violent headache.

Such are some of the beliefs, current or once current, in our county : but this branch of study requires a volume to itself in order to do it justice. In these few pages the subject is only glanced at, but its closer acquaintance will well repay the diligent student.

Northamptonshire Proverbs.

THE proverbs of Northamptonshire although not numerous are curious, and it will not be without interest to reproduce a few of the more historically interesting. It is an ancient saying :

"The Mayor of Northampton opens oysters with his dagger."

He is said to have done this to keep them a sufficient distance from his nose. Dr. Fuller says this "town being eighty miles from the sea, fish may well be presumed stale therein. Yet I have heard (says the Doctor) that oysters, put up with care, and carried in the cool, were weekly brought fresh and good to Althrop, the house of the Lord Spencer, at equal distance : and it is no wonder ; for I myself have eaten in Warwickshire, about eighty miles from London, oysters sent from that city, fresh and good ; and they must have been carried some miles before they came there."

There is an old Northampton saying respecting fuel :

"He that must eat a buttered faggot let him go to Northampton."

Fuller explains the origin of this proverb thus : " Because it is the dearest town in England for fuel, where no coals can come by water, and little wood doth grow on land." Camden noted the absence of trees in the county.

A couplet says :

> " Brackley breed,
>   Better to hang than to feed."

" Brackley," wrote Ray, " is a decayed market-town and borough, which abounding with poor, and troubling the country about with beggars, came into disgrace with its neighbours. I hear now that this place is grown industrious and thriving, and endeavouring to wipe off the scandal."

Morton mentions the next two that we give :

> " If we can Padwell overgoe, and Horestone we can see,
>   Then Lords of England we shall be."

" That there was a battle at Danesmore, betwixt the Saxons and the Danes, the name of the place, and constant tradition of the inhabitants, may reasonably incline us to believe. The people there have a notable rhime, which they make the Danes to say upon the point of battel. Padwell is a noted flush spring in Edgcote grounds. Horestone, a famous old stone upon the borders of Warwickshire (in Wardlington field)."

" Wansford, in England."

"Another, though less tragical, instance of the greatness and suddenness of the inundations of the Nyne, is that well-known and not unpleasant story of a man who, as he was fast asleep on a little haycock in a meadow on the Nyne, nigh Wansford, never dreaming either of floods or rain, was carry'd off by one of these floods, with his haycock under him. The poor man at length awakes, and looks about him with all the surprise imaginable. He had laid down to sleep on a haycock in a dry meadow nigh Wansford, but finds himself afloat in the midst of waters, for ought he knew, in the wide ocean ; and as the story goes, one espying him in this condition, calls to him, and enquires where he lived. The poor fellow in a piteous tone, reply'd, 'At Wansford, in England.' However, the memory of the accident is preserved in the sign of the chief inn at Wansford. And thence the common proverbial saying of, living at Wansford, in England ; so common hereabouts that I admire it escaped Mr Fuller in his collection of *Local Proverbs.*"

An Ancient Hospital.

BY REV. I. WODHAMS, M.A.

THE story of the Ancient Hospital of St. John and St. James, at Brackley, may not be so interesting as other stories which relate to "Bygone Northamptonshire," yet in some respects this Hospital, and the chronicles belonging to it, are unique. The chapel of the Hospital still exists, and relics of its antiquity remain in spite of various restorations following upon preceding neglect. Some beautifully-cut Norman moulding over the doorway, an unpolished Purbeck marble pillar of fine proportions in the north-west wall, the bowl of an early English font, several plain doorways and windows, an east window of great size, two stone figures, supposed to represent St. John and St. James, remain as witnesses of its past glories, and form part of the venerable building, which is still used, as of yore, for prayer, praise, and thanksgiving. The very stones are a link between the lives passed away and those of the coming generation. For a long time the chapel remained in ruins, now it is again used by Magdalen College School and the Parish of Brackley. Many of the buildings of its time have perished, or are in a state of picturesque ruin. This remains to connect a dead past with a living present.

Similarly, the Hospital, too, has come down to modern times, with its continuity more or less broken, from the twelfth century. Through various vicissitudes, which endangered its existence, some of local character, others arising from national ferment, the old foundation has been preserved, and its character and spirit remain almost unchanged. By curious processes, which have very slowly developed, the venerable institution has become a school—and no school in England, we believe, can trace its origin back to so early a period. More than 700 years have passed over it, and the present Magdalen College School may be said to be the child of the Oxford College of that name, and the grandchild of the primary foundation.

The founder was Robert, Earl of Leicester, called Robert "le Bossu," and who was the second of four Earls of Leicester of the same name. The date of the charter is not given, but from the character of the writing, and from known details of the founder, the date can be fixed approximately about the year 1160. The Earl of Leicester had previously founded the Abbey of St. Mary de Pré, the great house of Augustinian canons at Leicester. Being Lord of the Manor at Brackley, he granted an acre of land to " Solomon the Clerk," that he might build there a Hospital and a free chapel to be dedicated to St. John the Apostle. The freedom of the chapel was confirmed by the Abbot and monastery of Leicester, by the Bishop of Lincoln, in whose diocese Brackley then was, and by the Pope. This chapel was intended for use as a private chapel of the Earls of Leicester, when in residence at the Manor, as well as a chapel of the Hospital, and its freedom still remains. It is still independent of the Parish Church, except by the mutual consent of the vicar and the authorities of Magdalen College. The heart of Robert, Earl of Mellent, the father of the founder, was deposited in the chapel in lead. This circumstance is recorded in the chronicles of Knyghton, in the Cotton Library, " Robertus comes Mellenti venit cum Willielmo scilicet conquestare in Angliam.

Iste Robertus hospitale de Brackley fundavit, et
dotavit, ubi cor ejusdem, ad huc integrum in
plumbo, sale servatum, habetur."

The "ad huc" was, of course, about the end of
the fourteenth century.   The nineteenth century
proved too much for what was "integrum in
plumbo, sale servatum" in the fourteenth.   A
workman, in the year 1836, in digging a hole for
a gallery, found a leaden box.   Opening it, there
was revealed a "bit of old leather," and this he
threw away.

The Hospital probably had the same rule as
the Austin canons.   There were a master (or
prior, as he is sometimes called) and brethren,
not all in holy orders.   Only the master was
bound to be so;   probably the brethren were
mostly in minor orders;   there is no evidence to
show that they were other than "secular clerks."
The patrons of the Hospital were the Earls of
Leicester.   They presented the master (or prior),
gave grants of land to the master and brethren.
Amicia, a granddaughter of the founder, married
Simon de Montfort, and their son held a meeting
of the barons at Brackley, to formulate the
demands which they presented to King John at
Northampton.   The Manor of Brackley and the

patronage of the Hospital passed next to the De
Quincys, who were good friends to Brackley and
the Hospital. Roger de Quincy, Earl of
Winchester, granted a charter to the burgesses.
The heart of Margaret, Countess of Winchester,
was buried in the chapel, where also were laid
her son Roger and his two wives. By the side
of the shrine in which the heart of his mother lay
entombed, Earl Roger had placed a measure made
in the shape of a coffin, and provided that it
should be filled with corn from his Manor of
Hawes three times in the year, for the use of the
Hospital. The patronage passed after his death
to the family of the Zouches, thence by marriage
to the Hollands. Towards the end of the
fourteenth century, difficulties of various kinds
beset the Hospital, bad management, disputes
with their neighbours, and probably with their
patrons. When, through another heiress, the
Hospital came under the Lovels, the brethren,
who in 1279 numbered amongst them nine priests
beside the master, and who in 1381 were reduced
to a total of four, became extinct, and on the
death of John Brokehampton, in 1423, the
Hospital was left without inhabitants. Francis,
Lord Lovel (or "Lovel the Dog,") sold the

Hospital and its possessions to William of Waynflete, the founder of Magdalen College, and the old foundation was incorporated in that college. In the reign of King Henry VIII., the President and Fellows and Scholars made use of the buildings during a plague at Oxford, and they seem to have served as a temporary habitation of the college in other times of pestilence or scarcity. A chauntry priest was maintained by the college; the last was John Barnard, who had an annual stipend of £8 6s. 8d. On his death the college established a school; Thomas Godwin, afterwards Bishop of Bath and Wells, was probably the first master. Antony à Wood says that he resigned his fellowship, and left Oxford, because he could not get on with certain "Papists" at Magdalen. Francis Godwin, his son, in his book "De Præsulibus Angliæ," says, "Pontificiorum factione . . . nescio quid prædioli oblatum est modo scholæ moderationem vellet suscipere, abdicata Magdaleusi societate, quam conditionem libeuter accepit sub exitum regni Edwardi sexti." In Queen Mary's reign he had to leave the school, but, having taken the degree of Bachelor of Medicine, he supported himself by its practice. The school was carried on until 1787 in the building occupied by the Chantry Priest. In Leland's time there were several tombs of noblemen in the presbytery of the Chapel. Mr. John Welchman repaired the Chapel in 1745. Neglect and disuse again brought it to desolation, and it was restored again during the last thirty years. The buildings suffered from being let on long leases, and but little remains of the old buildings except the chapel. Mr. Thomas Bannister, a master of the school, was buried in the chapel as lately as the year 1821.

THE END

𝔍𝔫𝔡𝔢𝔵.

P

List of Subscribers.

Abel & Sons, Northampton (4 copies).
Addison, Rev. L., Gretton.
Adkins, Mrs. H. D., Springfield, Northampton.
Allen, E. G., 28, Henrietta Street, Covent Garden, London.
Anderson, Rev. G., F.R.H.S., Otterhampton.
Anderson, Jno., jr., 99, Nassau Street, New York.
Archer, Henry, Wellingborough.
Armstrong, C., Cambridge.
Atkinson, Rev. C. Chetwynd, M.A., Ashton-on-Mersey.

Bain, Jas., Public Library, Toronto.
Barker, Rev. C. R., Duston, Northampton.
Barker, E. F., Trinity College, Cambridge.
Barlow, Alfred, Kettering.
Barker, Frank, Holly Road, Northampton.
Barrett & Son, Daventry.
Barry, J., Cliftonville, Northampton.
Beattie, S., 18, Marriott Street, Northampton.
Becke, C. C., 20, Market Square, Northampton.
Becke, John, The Cedars, Northampton.
Bell, Wm., The Hull Press, Hull.
Bellamy, C. H., 97, Bishop Street, Alexandra Park, Manchester.
Berrill, F., Kettering.
Bethell, W., Rise Park (2 copies).
Bigge, Rev. H. J., Cottingham, Uppingham.
Bird, Thos., Kettering.
Bird, W. L., Daventry.
Blunsom, Mr., Northampton.
Boden, Rev. M. H., Naseby Vicarage, Rugby.
Bohn, Geo., Tranby Park.
Bolam, C., Boughton House, Kettering.
Bools, W. E., 7, Cornhill, London.
Booth, Richard, Brighton.
Bostock, R. C., West Norwood.
Boutflower, Rev. D. S., Newbottle Vicarage.
Briggs, A., Rawden Hall, Leeds.
Bromley, Charles, Goole.
Bull, F. W., Kettering.
Bullock, Rev. G. F., King's Sutton.
Burnell, G., Northampton.
Butlin, H., Rothwell,

Buttanshaw, Rev. F., M.A.. Cotterstock, Oundle.

Carter, E. R., Post Office, Southampton.
Cary-Elwes, V. D. H., The Hall, Great Billing.
Cartwright, T. L., Melville, Newbottle Manor, Banbury.
Cartwright, W. C., Aynhoe Park, Banbury.
Cardigan, Countess of, Deene Park, Wansford.
Caster, G. C., Market Place, Peterborough.
Causton, W. H., M.D., 365, King Street, Ravenscourt Park, W.
Chamberlain, Alfred, B.A., Hull.
Chamberlain, C. W., Rothwell.
Chamberlain, D. B., Rothwell.
Channing, F. A., M.P., Pytchley House, Kettering.
Clarke, Rev. R. D. L., King's Cliffe, Wansford.
Cockayne, G. E., F.S.A., College of Arms, London (two copies).
Cohen, E. E., Hull.
Colledge, W. S., Junr., Northampton.
Collet, Rev. E., M.A., Long Eaton.
Cook, J. W., 7, Mark Lane, London.
Cooper, Major Cooper W., Toddington Manor, Dunstable.
Cooper, Hy., 17, The Drapery, Northampton.
Cordingley, Jno. R., 10, Melbourne Place, Bradford.
Couchman, Rev. E. C., Sibbertoft.
Cove, G. Arkesden, Lawford, Northampton.
Cox, Rev. R. H., M.A., Hardingstone.
Cox, Retired Commander, R.N., Hardingstone.
Crick, W. D., 7, Alfred Street, Northampton.
Curwen, G. R., Salem, Mass.
Currie, H. W., Rushden House, Higham Ferrers.
Cuthbert, Miss, Marston St. Lawrence, Banbury.

Dain, H. B., 41, Waterloo Street, Birmingham.
Davis, S., Towcester.
Dempsey, J., Belvedere, Boone, County Illinois.
Dempsey, John, Chicago, Illinois.
Dorman, T. Phipps, Reincliffe House, Northampton (2 copies).
Dolben, Miss Mackworth, The Hall, Finedon.
Draper, Jno., Lancaster, Grant County, Wisconsin, U.S.A.
Draper, E., Primrose Hill, Northampton.
Dryden, Sir Henry, Bart., Canons Ashby, Byfield.
Du Boulay, Rev. J. H., East Haddon.
Durham, E. A., St. Andrew's Villa, Northampton.
Duthy, Miss, Islip, Thrapstone.
Dyer, H. H., 2, Newland, Northampton.

Eady, J. C., Market Harborough.
Edmonds, Rev. F. S., Harringworth.
Early, W. J., Wellingborough.
Ellcott, E. K., Towcester.
Elvin, C. N., M.A., Eckling Grange, East Dereham.
Egerton, B. de M., Brackley.
Empson, C. W., 11, Palace Court, Bayswater Hill, W.
English, M. Y., Orton, Peterborough.

Feather, Rev. G., Glazenbury Vicarage, Manchester.
Fennings, L., Northampton.
Fickling, W., St. Peter's College, Peterborough.
Fielder, E. J., 110, Brixton Road, London, S.W.
Firth, S., 4, Exchange Buildings, Leicester.
Foljambe, Cecil G. S., M.P., Cockglode, Ollerton.
Forster, T., Colchester.
Foster, Jos., Market Harborough.
Foster, W. H., Spratton Grange.
Frisby, S., Northampton.
Frost, Thomas, Derby.

Galloway, F. C., Bowness-on-Windermere.
Gardner, Arthur, Northampton.
Garrard, G. E., Northampton.
Gasquoine, Rev. T., Northampton.
Gates, H. P., J.P., The Vineyard House, Peterborough.
Gaylor, C., Brixworth.
Gibbs, A. J., Northampton.
Gibson, W. H., Northampton.
Gooch, Rev. Jno., Holcott, Northampton.
Gordon, Rev. C. J., Rushden, Higham Ferrers.
Gorman, D., Chesterfield.
Goss, W. E. and J., Kettering (2 copies).
Greene, R., F.R.C.P.E., Berry Wood.
Green, Thos., 20, Market Square, Northampton.
Gregory, M. W., Lellington Avenue, Leamington.
Gross, Rev. A. W., Milton (2 copies).
Guest, W. H., Arlington Place, 263, Oxford Road, Manchester.

Hadland, S., Lower Weedon.
Haggerston, W. J., Newcastle-on-Tyne Public Libraries (2 copies).
Hainsworth, L., 120, Bowling Old Lane, Bradford.
Halford, Rev. J. F., Brixworth.
Harding, S. J., Kettering.
Harrison, Rev. J. B., Paulerspury.
Harrison, J. H., Bugbrooke, Weedon.
Harold, F., Northampton.
Haslewood, Rev. F. G., LL.D., Chislet, Canterbury.
Hayes, Miss, Brafield.
Hesleden, B., Derngate, Northampton.
Hewlett, Miss A. M., 83, Bailiff Street, Northampton.
Higgins, Mrs. Jno. Knight, Northampton.
Hill, B. R., 19, Woodlands Terrace, Darlington.
Hill, Rev. Charles, M.A., Culworth.
Hill, F., Castilian Terrace, Northampton.
Holden, Rev. Canon, D.D., South Luffenham.
Holding, M., A.R.I.B.A., Northampton.
Hope, H. W., Luffness, Drem, N.B.
Hopkinson, Rev. F., LL.D., The Dell, Malvern Wells.
Horn, General Sir Frederick, G.C.B., Buckby Hall, Rugby.
Hull, C., 2, Albert Road, Regent's Park, London, N.W.
Humphreys, Rev. A. G. P., Thorpe, Mandeville.
Hunt, Miss, St. Rumbald's, Astrop, King's Sutton.
Huntingford, Rev. G. W., Barnwell, Oundle.

Hutchinson, H., Wythemail Park, Orlingbury.

Isham, Sir C., Bart., Lamport Hall.

Jacobson, Thos. E., Sleaford.
James, D., Burton Latimer.
James, F., Edgeworth Manor, Cirencester.
Jesson, Thos., F.G.S., Great Houghton House, Northampton.
Jeyes, Miss, Holly Lodge, Boughton.
Johnson, A., 47, Oxford Terrace, Hyde Park, W.

Kegan Paul, Trench, & Co., Paternoster House, London.
Kilburn, A. H., 8, Gold Street, Northampton.
Knightley, Lady, Fawsley, Daventry.
Kirby, Miss, Glapthorne, Oundle.
Kirby, J. W., Bozeat, Wellingborough.

Lane, C. W., Kettering.
Law, Rev. Wm. Marston, Trussell (2 copies).
Lea, Mrs., Northampton.
Leathes, F. de M., 17, Tavistock Place, W.C.
Linnell, W. H., Wootton Grange, Northampton.
Leggott, J. H., F.R.H.S., Stowmarket.
Legard, Rev. Cecil, Cottesbrooke.
Leicester, Lord Bishop of, Peterborough.
Lilford, Lord, Lilford Hall, Oundle.
Lindsay, Rev. H., Kettering.
Lloyd, H., Pitsford Hall, Northampton.
Loyd, Rev. L. H., Little Houghton (2 copies).

Mackintosh, Rev. A., Moulton.
Manfield, J., 62, Billing Road, Northampton.
Manfield, M. P., M.P., Northampton.
Markham, C. A., F.S.A., Sedgebrook, Northampton.
Markham, H. P., Court House, Northampton.
Marlow, Miss, 102, Abington Street, Northampton.
Maunsell-Tibbits, J. B., Barton Seagrave.
Mee, Mrs. E., 17, Mina Street, Llanelly.
Mills, R. M., Bourne.
Monkhouse, F., Kingston Mount, Didsbury.
M'Cormick, Rev. F. H. J., F.S.A., Scot, Ilkeston.
Moore, Rev. E. M., Benefield.
Mutton, J., Derngate, Northampton.

Newman, Rev. F. B., Burton Latimer.
Newman, W., M.D., Stamford.
Nicholson, Rev. Geo., B.A., Langham Place, Northampton (2 copies).
Nicholson, John, Hull.
Norman, D., Towcester.
Northampton Free Library.

O'Brien, H. S., Blatherwycke Park, Wansford.
Owen, Dr., Rushden, Higham Ferrers.

Packe, Rev. H. V., Lamport.
Page, J. T., Holmby House, Forest Gate.
Parkinson, J. A., Northampton.
Patchett, John, Mildred House, Undercliffe Lane, Bradford.
Payling, R., Cowgate, Peterborough.
Payne, W. G. Reeves, Northampton.
Paul, Rev. G. W., Finedon.
Penny, Rev. E. L., D.D., Plymouth.
Percival, Andrew, Minster Close, Peterborough.
Percival, T. M., Park House, Towcester.
Phillips, Rev. James, Weston Favell.
Phillips, M., West Street House, Chichester.
Pinder, James, Thornby Hall, Rugby.
Potts, John, *Guardian* Office, Banbury (2 copies).
Pratt, S., Stanwick House, Higham Ferrers.
Pressland, T., Dallington.
Prichard, H. S., Abington Abbey (2 copies).
Pulpher, Jabez, Raunds.

Ramsay, B., Brackley.
Randall, J., Bank Chambers, George Street, Sheffield.
Ratt, Geo., Rockingham.
Rawlins, Lt.-Colonel J., Earls Barton.
Robinson, H. A., Guildhall Road, Northampton.
Robinson, Ro., Handsworth, Birmingham.
Reynolds, D., 20, Margaret Street, Northampton.
Ross, Fredk., F.R.H.S., 137, Huddleston Road, Tufnell Park, N.
Rothwell Congregational Sunday School Library.

Scholes, Councillor, Morley.
Scratten, Rev. W., Badby.
Scriven, R. G., Castle Ashby.
Scott, Mrs., Clarenden Lodge, Hardingstone.
Severance, Miss, Thenford.
Sharman, Wm., Wellingborough.
Sheffield, D., Earls Barton.
Shepard, Thos., The Hill House, Kingsthorpe.
Simpson, William, 71A, St. Giles Street, Northampton (2 copies).
Sissmore, Rev. T. L., 31, Green Park, Bath.
Smith, Geo. T., Towcester.
Smith, H. H., Stanley Grove, Oxford Road, Manchester.
Smith, J.P., Rothwell.
Smith, Mrs. H., Alderton, Towcester.
Smith, Rev. S. L., Brampton Ash.
Spokes, Mrs. Elizabeth, Abington (2 copies).
Sotheby, Major-General, Ecton.
Stevenson, F., 104, Regent's Park Road, London, N.W.
Stewart, Rev. J., F.R.H.S., Penryn.
Stockdale, Henry M., Mears Ashby Hall.
Stringer, C. W., Southlands, Kettering.
Swallow, T. W., Northampton.
Swane, T., Keighley.
Sweeting, Miss S. E., 11, Bedford Well Road, Eastbourne.

Taylor, Rev. R. V., B.A., Melbecks, Richmond.
Teesdale, Eugene, Hull.
Thompson, Beeby, Northampton.
Thompson, Jno., J.P., The Lindens, Peterborough (2 copies).
Thorpe, C. E., 8, Billing Road, Northampton (2 copies).
Thursfield, J. F., Kettering.
Trolove, F. W., Rushton.
Tolhurst, Jno., Glenbrook, Beckenham.
Toller, T. N., M.A., 13, Mauldeth Road, Fallowfield, Manchester.
Tucker, Raymond, St. Margaret's Mansions, Victoria Street, London.
Turner, Rev. V. C., Little Oakley.
Tyack, Rev. G. S., B.A., Crowle.

Walls, Mr., Junr., Northampton.
Watson, Rev. J. S., Lowick, Thrapston.
Watson, G. L., Rockingham Castle.
Watts, J. W., Wollaston, Wellingborough.
Wells, Rev. H. W., Great Missenden, Bucks.
Wells, W. R., Northampton.
West, T. G., 9, Aberdeen Terrace, Northampton.
Whistler, Rev. R. A., M.A., Pilton, Oundle.
White, Rev. R. D., Moreton Pinkney, Byfield.
Wickes, Rev. J. B., M.A., Boughton, Rectory.
Wicksteed, Chas., Kettering.
Willes, W. A., King's Sutton Manor, Banbury.
Wildridge, F., Silver Street, Wellingborough.
Wildridge, T. Tindall, Beverley.
Wilkinson, W. King, M.A., Whiteholme, Slaidburn, Clitheroe.
Wilson, Rev. W., Stoke, Bruerne.
Wing, Rev. C. Foston, Wigston, Leicester.
Wrighton, W. E., 19, Helen Street, Woolwich.
Wodhams, Rev. I., M.A., Brackley.
Wood, R. H., F.S.A., Penrhos House, Rugby (4 copies).
Wood, Rev. W. S., Alfford, Stamford.
Woolston, T. H., Kingsley Road, Northampton.

Yates, Rev. W., M.A., Cottingham Rectory, Uppingham.